# Professors and Other Inmates

# Professors and Other Inmates

STUDENT X

ARLINGTON HOUSE · PUBLISHERS
NEW ROCHELLE, N. Y.

Manufactured in the United States of America

**Library of Congress Cataloging in Publication Data**

Student X
Professors and other inmates.

1. College students--United States--Personal narratives. 2. College students--Recreation. I. Title.
LA229.S74 371.8'0973 74-13394
ISBN 0-87000-240-6

# Dedication

This book is dedicated to my favorite English literature instructor. Not because he was a great instructor, or even a good one, but because his ability to take a reasonably interesting subject and reduce it to complete insignificance and present it with such inspired indifference never ceased to amaze me.

# Contents


Introduction . . . . . 9
1 Dropping Out . . . . . 11
2 Dropping Back In . . . . . 23
3 Preenrollment . . . . . 27
4 Enrollment . . . . . 29
5 Student Housing . . . . . 37
6 Professors . . . . . 47
7 Lecturers . . . . . 61
8 Running the Course . . . . . 71
9 Administration . . . . . 105
10 It Pays to be Black . . . . . 107
11 If All Else Fails, Read the Instructions . . . . . 109
12 Student Dorms . . . . . 113
13 Getting High . . . . . 115
14 The First Week of School . . . . . 119
15 Graduate School . . . . . 135
Conclusion . . . . . 137

# Introduction

Several friends suggested that I was not capable of writing this book and secretly I suspected they were correct. It was not until members of the faculty came around and pointed out my gross incompetence in writing this book. . . . "or any other book," that I decided to proceed.

Generally speaking, professors have more theories than a cat has fleas. And those theories are of about as much value to him as the fleas are to the cat.

# 1
# Dropping Out

My retreat from the academic community was astonishingly abrupt. The reason for the hasty departure is not likely to grow dim or doubtful in the next two or three millennia. Surprisingly enough, however, this sudden decision to terminate my formal education had nothing to do with the physical condition of any of the coeds in residence. It happened like this: Science, any possible kind of science, even in its remotest forms, even political science, has never been my strong suit. The arts, being easier, less precise, and thus more adapted to the simple-minded, were my better subjects. So, for my first three semesters I studiously avoided any of the various types of the dismal sciences. Unbeknownst to me, the university had its fatherly eye on my future, and one day there appeared in my mail box an urgent notice to see my adviser without further delay. In those days a note of such magnitude overshadowed every other piece of mail—with the notable exception of those depressing brown envelopes saying "Department of the Army."

I put that visit off so long I began to worry that the Establishment might have a warrant out for my arrest. Finally, not being able to sleep any longer, I made my way over to my adviser's office. That is, *he* called it an office, though it had an amazing resemblance to a broom closet. The furnishings, in any other room, would have been sparse, yet under the circumstances they must have had to grease that old desk and use a large pry-bar in order to get it into the designated space.

The adviser made a gesture I interpreted to mean "have a seat," as he tickled the innards of an ancient and fragrant "oom-paul" pipe with a much-used pipe cleaner. The gesture amazed me, as I was not aware that another chair existed, and I was surprised that I could have missed it in such crowded quarters. A quick reinspection verified my first observation that aside from *his* chair, which was abundantly occupied, his desk and a 1921 model of Webster's *New Collegiate Dictionary* were the only other furnishings aside from a varied assortment of water and sewer lines that wandered aimlessly through the room apparently in no particular pattern and obviously in no hurry to get wherever they were supposed to go. One of these pipes, situated at approximately the correct height and having a worn and much-used appearance, seemed the most likely spot for me to park my, er, posterior. Presence of mind and a guardian angel caused me to reach out and check the temperature of that innocent-looking pipe before I used it for a perch. That one small caution is the only reason I'm not wearing a permanent brand from that cow college to this day. That unwrapped, unprotected steampipe was simply throbbing with the urge to impress me.

Quietly I said I believed I would stand if it was all right with the adviser. He raised two stubby eyebrows that resembled worn-out paint brushes and nodded his approval, as if to say "one of the bright ones, huh?" His eyes were busy inspecting me, apparently very intently, as he stoked that huge old pipe with a fistful of tobacco and proceeded to tromp it down with a pudgy finger.

"What's your name, son?" he asked, as he searched himself for a light. I told him. There was a blank stare for just an instant, but his fingers never broke stride in their diligent search for a light. His grey eyes slowly began to narrow, and it was impossible to tell if my name brought to mind some sinister plot of which I was unaware, or whether he was only concerned about finding a light.

Presently he produced three large kitchen matches. Striking all three at once, he held them in a practiced manner and set fire to that bale of stems and straw he considered tobacco. Perhaps it was tobacco. Probably some foreign brand. But the stench reminded me of my younger days on the farm when we used to burn the fencerows, which consisted mostly of sunflowers and green tumbleweeds. In that confined area it was hard to take. I breathed as little and as seldom as possible. It did seem that we were in the midst of a full-fledged catastrophe, yet I remained quiet and suffered in silence. Once he had that old "widow-maker" of a pipe fairly well belching along, he leaned back, his eyes closed drowsily, and he looked as content as a python who had just eaten a whole flock of chickens—henhouse and all.

"Well, what's your problem—er, Sonny?" The paunchy old fogey, he'd forgotten my name already. I explained that I didn't know *what* the problem was and produced the well-worn, soiled, and dog-eared slip of paper I had received. He glanced over it, then with a bit of a surprise said, "why, this note is almost two months old!"

"Yes sir."

"Why didn't you come in earlier?" I never did like to be pinned down that way.

"I had a grandmother in the hospital," I lied.

"Oh, and she died, of course," he said with immense sarcasm.

"No sir," I replied quietly.

"Well, I'm relieved to hear that," he said, continuing the sarcasm.

"She had triplets."

Lord, it did hit him hard, but he got himself together quickly and gave me a black look. Senior members of the academic community do not like to be out done by a smartass sophomore. It looks bad.

"I seem to recall, now," he was saying, "something about your particular problem. Let's see now . . ." He puffed thoughtfully at that deadly pipe, and began that familiar professional shuffle of the three or four hundred pieces of unorganized paper that littered his desk. "Ah, yes. Here it is . . . well, well, well, . . . uhuh, . . . hum-m-m." Obviously only one of us was getting any information, worthwhile or otherwise. Between us we had already breathed all the available air in the room three or four times each, and my lungs were threatening to go on strike.

"Wha—what seems to be the matter?" I wheezed.

"It's a serious problem we have here. Very serious."

Right at the moment I couldn't imagine anything much more serious than my immediate health. I took a deep breath, then waited for my vision to clear somewhat, and asked, "what is the *other* serious problem?"

"It appears," he began, "that you have not been acquiring the proper number of courses in the sciences. You cannot hope to escape, er, I mean *graduate* without the required number of hours in the various fields of science to round out your education. Let's see here . . . you'll need some chemistry, and a course in biological science, no, . . . better make that zoology. . . ."

"That's great," I thought, "just when I'm dying for a breath of fresh air he turns up with verbal diarrhea!

". . . and a little calculus."

CALCULUS! . . . . Hell, sir, I can barely add! I took trigonometry twice in high school and didn't even learn how to *spell* it! . . . . Why in the Board of Regents' name does an *English* major need *calculus?"*

I was malevolently ignored as he continued to plot my doom.

I was two weeks recovering from the near fumigation. By that time a new semester had begun, and I had found myself in zoology lab and face-to-face with a plump mouse cadaver. Being a farm boy, I was in complete agreement that the only good mouse is a dead mouse. So I picked him up by his slender tail and headed for the door. My intention, and I still think it was a good one, was to throw him out, but I was stopped on the way by a laboratory assistant.

"Where you going wiz zee leetle mouze?" the foreign graduate assistant inquired.

"Why, I'm gonna throw him out," I said.

"And what, may I ask, ees wrong weez heem?"

"Wrong with . . . he happens to be dead! That's primarily what's wrong with him." These stupid foreigners; you have to explain everything to them.

"Precisely," he replied.

" . . . Precisely, what?" I asked.

"Hee's dead."

"Yeah, I thought you'd see it my way."

"You would not prefer to work on heem *alive,* would you?"

"*Work* on him?" I asked, a suspicion slowly growing on me.

"Certainly. Eet deed not escape your most observant eye, deed eet not, zat each of zee ozers in zee class also have zemselves a mooze?"

"Wha—, er no. Certainly not. What are we supposed to *do*

with the—?"

"Eef you had read ze manual as you are supposed to have do before coming to ze class, you would know zat you are to dizect ze mooze und observe ze location of ze heart, lungs, and ozzer organs und draw zeem off on ze chart in ze manual."

It was gonna be worse than I expected. The humiliation of operating on a mouse. But the worst was yet to come!

Each person was assigned a lab partner. There were two freshmen girls, twirlers in the band, and a few other attractive young creatures in the class, but as luck would have it, I drew a hulking junior-college transfer football player with the highly appropriate name of Harry Buffalo. Harry had the biggest arms I've ever seen in captivity—and the smallest brain ever recorded on either side of captivity.

Things settled down somewhat as everyone plunged into the lab manual he was supposed to have read before coming to class, or bent over his little specimens.

After eyeing my lab manual for some minutes, I had discovered that I was to find a dissecting kit in a small drawer underneath the counter. There I found the kit. "Now, lemme see, it says take the mouse, put him on his back, and make an incision from his breast bone all the way back to his . . . well, that's strange enough . . . where'd the mouse go?. . . . Was here just a couple of minutes ago. Couldn't have run off. Dead. No question 'bout that . . . was even getting a little stiff . . . . Got to be 'round here somewhere. Now, where the hell could . . . ? That mouse Harry's working on. It has a black spot on its side . . . *my* mouse had a black spot on its side just like that . . . . *Harry, that's my mouse you've got there.*"

"No, my mouse."

"No, Harry, you're mistaken. That is my mouse. He has a black spot on his side and that one is mine . . . Yours must be around here somewhere."

"No. This my mouse," he turned slightly away from me.

"I'm really sorry, Harry, but that is MY mouse," I said in a firm voice.

"No. This is my mouse!"

"Harry, GIMME MY GODDAMN MOUSE!"

My streaking hand scooped up the mouse at the same instant that Harry's huge paw clamped down on my wrist. I thought the blood was going to squirt out of the end of my fingers. But I had to hang on. It was a matter of pride now. Harry's face was close to mine. It's the only face I've ever seen where the eyebrows and the hairline met. That low forehead and those beady bloodshot eyes glaring at me. I looked at Harry. I looked at the mouse. "Ten seconds ago," I thought, "there was nothing I wanted so bad . . . suddenly I'd give twenty dollars to be rid of the friggin thing!"

"Here! Here! What eez going on here?" It was the tenor voice of the little foreign lab assistant whom I had despised so thoroughly a few minutes ago. God, how great it was to see a human face again!

"You, ah, gentlemen seem to be having some difficulty wiz ze assignment, no?"

"Well, yes, it would seem so." I replied as calmly as I could under the circumstances. "Right now we have *two* problems. Firstly, I'm about to lose a hand from lack of circulation and, secondly, Harry, here, absconded with my mouse."

"Mr. Buffalo, did you take hees mooze?"

"No. My mouse."

"Aw, Shutup, Harry!" I said. It had suddenly occurred to me why Dear Harry was my lab partner. I was on an athletic scholarship also, and had made good grades in the lesser disciplines, and it had been decided to saddle me with poor ole' Harry to get him through.

We finally persuaded Harry to spring my arm, but he got to keep the mouse. He was welcome to him. To this day, I believe he *ate* that first mouse! Whatever, I was soon back at work trying to identify properly the various plumbing and mechanical parts of a deceased mouse, for I unfortunately had been supplied with yet another of the beasts.

Presently, it occurred to me to check on the progress Harry was making. Harry wasn't constructed for such delicate work as surgery on a mouse. It would have been better to have given him a dead mule and an axe. That poor mouse, what there was left, looked like he had clobbered it with a sledgehammer. It was plain to see Harry was going to have a tough time in this class.

The next day dawned bright and clear, so I was informed. On a happiness scale of one-to-ten, sunrise gets a minus-four on my chart. Anyway, the early hours held no clue to the depressing times ahead.

The dorm breakfast wasn't bad; cold gamey bacon; cold soggy toast; one rubber egg with all the resiliency of a kicking tee, and a sort of gooey sap reported to be coffee. That was the kind of sad farce perpetrated by dorm cafeterias as food. It didn't deceive anyone.

About the middle of the morning I managed to navigate over to the "nonprofit" Student Center where I procured yet another cup of ooze and grit referred to as coffee (12 cents), and consumed two sugar-coated donut holes (10 cents each). With this cargo stowed precariously aboard I wandered off in search of Simpleton Hall (halls are usually named after distinguished members of the faculty or administration) to partake of my first hour of calculus.

I found the classroom where this calculus was to take place. It was an uninspiring room, as classrooms usually are. I selected a seat near the rear of the room because I didn't want to appear too conspicuous. I had glanced through my textbook; it wasn't much help in clarifying the subject. There was occasionally a curious mention of something called "logarithms." I was not aware that raw timber had any particular musical beat, so I awaited the beginning of class with some interest.

It was not a winning situation. First, the instructor was a disappointment. He was approximately five foot-two, and wouldn't have weighed over a hundred and five. He sported a crew cut, a pair of glasses apparently ground from the bottoms of coke bottles, and an assorted collection of oversized teeth situated in such a manner that he could have eaten an apple through a knothole. His posture, what there was of it, was sad.

The instructor called roll and that was the last thing I understood that hour. I might as well have been in a foreign language class. Nor could I make any headway out of the strange hieroglyphics he kept drawing on the board.

My only gratification as I left the class was that I was not confused. In order to be confused one must have *some* knowledge of the subject so that he will have something to be confused *with*. But my ignorance was complete. It was absolutely untarnished. The academic fog was beginning to settle in.

I checked the schedule and my blood pressure dropped forty

points—*chemistry!* There didn't seem to be any way out of it, so I forced myself over to the chemistry classroom. Beginning chemistry classrooms were placed in cheaply-made tin quansets. These glorified rabbit hutches were placed off to the side, away from the main part of campus. It was presumed, by those unfortunates who labored in these stuffy sweatboxes, that they were so located in case some idiot should brew up the wrong concoction and thus suddenly distribute the immediate real estate over a larger area. Roll was called and each student was assigned a particular place to work. It was at this time that I realized my luck was indeed running on the negative side that semester. My lab partner was, of course—Harry Buffalo. One does what one can under whatever circumstances, so I was determined to make the best of this obviously trying situation.

There was a twenty-minute lecture by an exceedingly overweight spinster who was hibernating in middle age. As she waddled up and down the aisles her posterior gyrations reminded me of two beavers wrestling under a carpet. Her cropped salt-and-pepper hair seemed to have been styled by Zeus, god of lightning and thunder.

She assured us there were absolutely no dangers involved in beginning chemistry classes. We were also informed that anyone caught not wearing safety goggles would receive an automatic F. We were instructed on the use of fire extinguishers, which were scattered about the room. Then we were shown how to use a water hose to wash down a student, should he be in the vicinity of an acid explosion. Being paired with Harry, it was gratifying to know that I was not in danger from any of these possibilities.

The various pieces of equipment were patiently explained to us. We were advised that it was imperative to learn how to bend glass tubing because we would be contriving our own experiments.

A bunsen burner, one of those little open flame jobs, was lit and Big Bertha proceeded to demonstrate how to heat a piece of glass tubing and do the most creative things with it. Nothing to it. Mere child's play. We were now allowed to light our own little torches and experiment with the intricacies of tube-bending.

I remember turning on the gas. I also remember going

through the motions of striking the match. I remember it so particularly well because it was followed by such a splendid explosion. As I fell I couldn't help noticing a wicked ball of fire boiling toward the ceiling—directly over Harry's burner.

As I lay there, stunned, I wondered how poor Harry had done. My benumbed condition was not prolonged. One cannot remain indifferent to the frosty blast from a fire extinguisher, and I did not do so very long. Thrashing and scrambling, I regained my feet. Three things I was positive about: 1. the very marrow was frozen in my bones; 2. the place was hopelessly afire, and—wait a minute—blind?

"Help! I'm blind! I can't see anything! Somebody get me outa' here!" I began running and smashing into things. I heard glass breaking.

"Everyone's gone! I gotta find my way outa here by myself!" I dashed in another direction, collided with something solid, heard more glass shatter. I must be bleeding all over. Got to find that door! Took off in another direction and was grabbed bodily and lifted off the floor, My first mental reaction was, "Harry's okay."

Someone removed my goggles, which were covered with foam, and I could see again! How wonderful it was. There was Harry holding me like you would hold a wet cat. There was Big Bertha with the fire extinguisher—and over there, still in a state of shock, was the poor fellow who had been working on the other side of Harry. In his hand was the tube of glass he had been working on; his shirt, what was left of it, was smoldering; his hair, on one side, was singed almost to the scalp; the remaining side was standing bolt upright; and wisps of smoke were wafting out of his ears. Foam dripped from his nose and elbows. He hadn't moved since I struck that eventful match. An offensive smell of burnt hair hung in the air. We pulled ourselves together, and tried to reconstruct what had happened. It was apparent a burner had been on for some time. It was also obvious *whose* burner it was. While Big Bertha had been explaining the equipment to the class, Harry had been busy exploring things for himself, as kiddies are inclined to do. In the process, Harry had turned on his burner. When nothing happened, he went on to other more interesting pieces of equipment. For instance: he still had a test tube stuck on one finger.

Just previous to the blast Harry had conveniently disappeared to get another armful of glass tubing to play with.

Upon my suggestion the class agreed to kill him, but we couldn't decide who was going to carry out the sentence.

Harry and I had a little talk, in which I cussed him for everything I could think of. I was discreet enough to do it in French, however, and Harry probably thought it was all a billet-doux. Harry was big-hearted and generous that way. It would have been some improvement for society if a little less heart and a few more brains had been employed in his construction.

I asked Harry to watch me and do only as I did and perhaps we *might* survivive the afternoon. After checking to be sure his burner was turned off, I lit mine. Then I lit his and told Harry to watch. "Try to follow instructions."

I cut each of us a piece of glass tubing. We held these in the hot little flame until they began to melt. I checked mine but it wasn't quite ready for my artistic efforts and was returned to the fire. Soon it had that nice rosy glow and, under modest pressure, it curved around into a neat right-angle bend. Gee, but that was easy! Maybe this class won't be such a drag after all. I laid that piece down to cool and picked up another short length of tubing to continue this fascinating practice.

I molded a few more bends and loops and even tried a couple of spirals. It wasn't beautiful work, like the girl across the desk was doing, but it was passable and would serve the purpose well enough.

Harry had enough melted and twisted tubing over there to go into the neon-sign business. It was about time I gave some of this work a closer inspection. I reached down and picked up the first piece of tubing I had worked with. I was examining it carefully when a strange, nauseous sensation came over me. It was unnerving. The smell of burning flesh wafted upward and waves of pain needled my fingers and moved swiftly up to my elbow. I tried to let go of the white-hot tubing but it was melted into the pores of my fingers and fused with the flesh. I took my other hand and pried it loose. There was a round canyon in the thumb and first two fingers of my left hand. The skin was black with a sort of greenish cast. I could see it distinctly; even through the tears. I remember thinking it would have been pretty, in a morbid sort of way, if the pain would just go away.

But the pain didn't go away. It increased violently with every throb.

As I held my hand under the faucet and tried not to cry, I realized what had happened. Harry had done it to me again. He had laid his own piece of hot tubing down and picked up mine to examine it. Thinking it was my tube, I had picked it up. The water didn't help. Tears didn't help. *Nothing* helped! Taking out my handkerchief, I wet it and gently wrapped it around the burned fingers. Quietly I made my way to the exit.

Once outside in the sunlight, I uncovered the finger stubs and had another look. It wasn't pleasant. "Better see if they will ever work again," I thought. As I stretched my charred fingers, the skin cracked open and blood trickled over my hand. Rewrapping the hand, I walked slowly back to the dorm and, with the remaining good hand, packed my belongings. The humiliation was overwhelming.

"Damn that Harry," I thought. "He furnished too much variety for anybody but a well insured cat!" I pointed the car north, determined to leave the academic world to those more hardy and courageous.

# 2
# Dropping Back In

Ten years later I was sitting outside a plush motel on the shores of Lake Superior, watching the giant grain and ore freighters as they jockeyed into position to slip under the ancient high-lift bridge and into the Duluth harbor. It was a pleasant evening. The sun was setting in a wondrous blaze of golds and ochres, with here and there a masterful flush of red or orange to heighten the illusion that the world was at peace. Never, I believe, had I been so contented. A fat lazy old tabby came over and curled up in my lap as if to assure me that things were indeed as peaceful as they seemed. We sat there, the cat and I, and watched that magnificent scene and listened to the assorted horns and signals as those 700-foot freighters (nineteen in sight) waited impatiently for their turn to ease through the slip and into the harbor.

The splendor of the sunset slowly faded into the delicate pinks, soft violets and dusky purples that herald the dark. Night descended like a velvet curtain and a gentle breeze wafted in from the lake. It was cold. I pulled my light jacket closer and the cat departed, probably seeking a warmer lap. It was Labor Day, and Mother Nature was telling us it was the end of summer in the North Country. Tomorrow all the kiddies would be starting back to school. School. Funny how this time of year always brings back memories of school. Meeting old friends, making new acquaintances, the unfamiliar smell of new clothes, new textbooks, or the odor of old books that had been stored in a warm room all summer. Every fall nostalgia gets a grip on me and I have that urge to return to school. To the carefree days when worries were few and good times were easy to find. Girls didn't care whether you had much money in your pocket or not.

School was fun. For most of us those were the happiest days of our lives. I sat there and remembered until the chill began to congeal the morrow in my bones and I was forced to retire to warmer quarters.

It was an attractive room but somewhat melancholy. It was altogether appropriate for my nostalgic reflections. Settling down in a comfortable chair, I began to review my last ten years. I recalled how my father reacted when I told him I was going on the road as a photographer of executives. He is a frugal man of Scotch ancestry, and finally he said:

"Son, why don't you take up something with a bit more promise to it. Had you given any thought to becoming a freelance mortician?"

My father has a way with subtle sarcasm. But photography had been good to me, and the past several years I had also been writing steadily for the nation's finest fishing magazine. Life had been agreeable enough. There had even been time to stop for a semester here and there and take a few classes. Yet one grows tired of the constant travel and moving. Nine and a half years, mostly on the road, and where did that road lead? Perhaps another nine and a half years of the same? That didn't sound like much fun. But where would it end? The grave? Where does one stop? Where does one get off? What could I do if I did change professions? What were the alternatives?—Alternatives? *Why, I could go back to school!*

The next morning I awakened with a new perspective on life. Things were fun again. The plans, the preparations for going back to college. What would it be like at age 30? Would it be fun? Would it be a drag? How much had college life really changed in ten years? These thoughts and many more scrambled for position in my mind as I checked out of the motel, hooked onto my bass-boat, and departed for warmer latitudes. As long as I could go to college anywhere I wanted, it wasn't going to be up here in eskimo country where I had to tromp around in snow up to here, and freeze my tail off! But wherever, I had to get enrolled in a hurry.

Two days later I rolled into my little home town and dropped the news on my somewhat surprised parents. My father wrinkled his brow, let the corners of his mouth settle disapprovingly—for effect—and pondered this new information.

Then he said:

"You might as well go back to school, son. You've avoided honest employment this long. Obviously you have talent—you've managed to stay out of jail all this time."

So it was that my college career began anew.

# 3

# Preenrollment

Getting into a major university as a freshman can be difficult. There are batteries of tests of various sorts, high school grades to be considered, perhaps even letters of recommendation, depending on the school. This is not really to weed out the boobs, as there is no college or university in existence that could survive without what is referred to as the *average student*. Rather, the process of getting enrolled is designed to weed out the student who is too aggressive, too eager, and might thus cause problems.

Perhaps you are not entirely familiar with how the university came into being, so I shall enlighten you. In the Middle Ages (I see no reason to clutter up this book with dates and names. It would only add an air of scholarly wisdom totally out of place in a volume about academic affairs) before the printing press, ignorance was an abundant commodity; most everyone had plenty to spare. In those remote times ignorance was as common as sex —sex and lice. Still, there were, here and there, men who were acclaimed as scholars in their field. The human race being what it is, one man cannot have something precious very long before another man thinks he wants some of it. That man will buy it if he can. If he cannot buy it he'll steal it. If he cannot steal it, he'll endure the most exquisite torture to get it.

That being the case, the scholars of the time, needing a way to make a living, and not being inclined to work (the early trend still prevails), set up classes which aspiring young scholars could attend for a small fee. There being no textbooks to convey the knowledge, the classroom lecture was born. It was the custom for the scholar to stand and read his notes while the class tediously copied the information. With all the scientific advancements in countless fields, you can still step into any classroom and find the same dull process: a dreary lecturer droning on before a classroom full of students scribbling notes.

When the scholar of the Middle Ages had finished reading his wearisome lecture, and the student had laboriously copied it, the student was then proclaimed a scholar in his own right. As a teacher he reread these copied notes to still more students. You can check any college of education in the world; the process has not changed appreciably. As you can see, the academic community is not prepared to cope with the nonconformist, the aggressive student, the eager student, the impatient student—the bright student.

It was Harry Truman who said he didn't want everyone to have a chance to go to college. If everyone went to college, then who would hire the college graduate? Be that as it may, the university system has been handed down to us more or less intact. It is the best we have, so we must abide by its antiquated rules or suffer at the hands of a modern society.

But colleges and universities are not as secure as they were a few years ago. The war babies have exited and enrolments are showing a noticable drop. And the country is awaking to the fact that society is becoming *ever-educated.* Advanced education begins to take on questionable significance when the Avon Lady has a degree in elementary education, and the fry-cook at Joe's Diner has his framed Ph.D. in engineering hanging above the grill.

While it may still be somewhat precarious for a freshman with a C average on his high school transcript to enlist at a major university, it is positively no trouble for an aging sophomore to invade the campus. The customary attitude of the college or university is that anyone over twenty-five has been sufficiently bruised by frequent bouts with society, and life in general, and is no longer any kind of threat to the organization. They were not prepared for anyone who had worked for himself, understood competence, and was a born reformer. So it was I found myself involved in the dispiriting process of enrollment—again.

# 4

# Enrollment

There is some difference between getting enrolled in college and being inducted in the army. Most colleges refrain from issuing uniforms. Otherwise the harassment is basically the same.

First, you must have a transcript of your grades, either from your high school, if you are a freshman, or from the college where you last attended. This transcript will cost you, on the average, five dollars for a Xerox copy. You pay the five dollars only to find the transcript is not valid unless the previous university has stamped the document with its official *seal,* and it must be signed by some underling in the registrar's office. For this stamping and signing you will probably stand in line an indefinite period and it is certain you will be allowed to contribute another sum, usually around twenty dollars.

You must not forget a withdrawal slip (approximately five dollars) and an official card of withdrawal (another three to five dollars).

At this point, most academic asylums begin to run out of ideas on how to fleece the departing student still further. You have paid your bail and you are free to go. All this has taken more time than expected. Upon returning to the car there are three tickets for overparking. After you have paid these, you are qualified to enroll at another university.

Once on the new campus you are directed to the office of the registrar, who, in turn, directs you to the office of admissions.

"Fine. Where is the office of admissions?" I asked the secretary.

"You're new on campus?"

"No Ma'am. I've been here twenty or thirty minutes already. It's just that I never knew where the admissions office was."

"Do you know where the chemistry building is?" she sighed.

"No, I'm afraid not," I replied.

"Do you know where building two-forty-three is?"

"You've got me again, lady."

"Well, let's see. Do you know where the library is?"

We stared at one another for a few moments. Finally I broke the silence.

"Do you happen to have a map of the campus?" I asked, hopefully.

"No sir, but you can get one at the Student Center," she replied.

"Great," I said, "where is this Student Center?"

She ushered me out the door and pointed across the campus green to a modernistic building with a sign that read "Student Center." She offered to walk me across the green to be sure I got there, but I detected a note of sarcasm and said no. It was a nice clear day and I believed if I took a bead on the place and didn't take my eyes off it that I could find it without further help. I thanked her and departed.

At the Student Center I located an information desk and asked for a campus map. Unless reason has deserted me, I believe campus maps must be contracted by a company specializing in such atrocities and drawn by a party or parties who have never set foot on the campus. Otherwise, why is it that even the oldest residing inmate on campus cannot look at a campus map and tell where he is, or show you how to get wherever it is you wish to go? Campus maps are not entirely useless: they make good placemats. The smaller ones serve as passable bookmarks.

By a tedious process of elimination, I found the office of admissions. There I filled out two forms in triplicate. They took one of the two copies of my transcript and twenty dollars. My next step was back at the office of the registrar where I filled out more forms, in triplicate, deposited the last copy of my transcript and got fleeced for five more dollars. From there they sent me to the office of records where I began to get some valuable experience in the art of standing in line. I had not been aware that I needed any practice to stand in line. I do readily admit that even with all the practice I received in the army, I was never able to stand line by myself, yet with only two or three others to help I have always been able to stand in line as patiently and persistently as anybody. It even seemed like I once took a course in line-standing but perhaps I am mistaken.

From registrar to records; from records to bursar's office. Meanwhile I had to retreat to the registrar's office to pick up the last copy of my transcript and have more duplicates made; return a copy to the registrars; scatter copies at the other stops; fill out acres of papers and distribute a bushel of five, ten and twenty dollar bills.

Eventually the university ran out of inventions for collecting preenrollment fees and the inevitable question arose:

"What college would I be enrolling in?"

"I thought I just enrolled," I said.

"No, sir. You only preenrolled. What 'college' do you wish to enroll in?" she asked.

I was very tired and not a little disgusted. In five hours I had been back and forth numerous times between seven buildings.

"I don't believe I understand," I sighed.

"Well, the university is divided into different schools," she said. "There is the school of engineering, the school of education, the school of home economics and so on. Now each school is called a col—"

"Oh, yes. I recall now. How stupid of me. Well, put me down for one."

She looked mystified; vagueness seemed to descend over her eyes.

". . . I beg your pardon, sir?"

"You may put me down for a college," I said in a simple and somewhat disinterested voice.

"Which *one?"* She looked nervous. It's not normal for someone to make problems. The theory is to keep the students confused until they get to class, at which point the administration can depend on the professors to mesmerize them. Thus there are seldom any uprisings or insurrections. It insures peaceful coexistence and few problems. But this young lady felt she was losing control of the situation. Something had gone amiss. Her job might even be in danger. Standard operating procedure is supposed to insure safety to each university employee. The employee is firmly instructed to ask only certain questions to which he should receive stock replies. If a student asks a question to which the employee has no answer, the student is referred to another office, in a different building. If it is a particularly sticky question which no one is anxious to field, this referral process can, at a major university, continue until the student gives up in disgust, or grows infirm with age. Either way the university wins.

Yet here was a most perplexing situation. The student had asked no unusual questions; had not misbehaved in any way; was polite enough; what to do?

"You choose one," I answered.

". . . I can't do *that!*" she cried.

"Why not?"

". . . Well, well, sir, you're *supposed* to know what the hell it is you want to do when you get this far along!"

This was my first encounter with the liberated female tongue. It took me somewhat by surprise. Anyway, she had spotted me for what I was; dangerous game. Time to ease up.

"Okay," I shrugged, "put me down for Arts and Sciences."

She looked immensely relieved.

Following more general directions, I found my next port of call, which was, naturally, the dean's office for the college of Arts and Sciences. Once I had made another five dollar deposit toward the remainder of my education, I was assigned an adviser.

The principal purpose of advisers is, not surprisingly, to advise. Yet there seem to be certain prerequisites that one must meet before he can become an adviser. First, he must not dress in any manner that might conform. Second, have a commanding vocabulary of obscure terms; third, have bad breath; fourth, have a background as far removed from the one in which he is counseling as possible. I recall a friend in electrical engineering who had an adviser from the botany department whose specialty was conifers of the Sahara region, or something like that.

When one is being advised by an adviser, one is expected to accept every word as something approaching Holy Writ. To question the word of an adviser is to antagonize. Many advisers, when in the intimate presence of a student, exude the aura of some small diety. The simplest question is considered a serious affront to their intelligence (which it probably is). The merest suggestion that you might have some ideas of your own as to what you would prefer to study will often send an adviser into a tantrum, or he will put down his pen and pout, or suggest that perhaps *you* would like to fill out your *own* schedule. This implies that the student does not have the intelligence to fill out his own schedule and does not know what is good for him. Last but not least, the adviser knows that the schedule is not legal until he has initialed it. Translated this means: "sit down, shut up, and don't sway the ship. Otherwise there will be frost on the bananas before I initial your schedule."

Of late, this attitude hasn't been working so well. It is getting harder and harder for the unimaginative and listless adviser to intimidate students. Especially the brighter, more aggressive student. The administration might be mildly surprised to know how many schedules are initialed S.I.M. which, decoded, means—Signed It Myself! I can testify that such schedules clear the registrar's office as swiftly as the others.

My adviser was all I expected, which wasn't much: paunchy, vapid, indifferent, humorless, and unimaginative. All advisers are not born with these fine qualities: they acquire them from the dreariness of the job, and association with peers who have these traits refined to an admirable degree. Occasionally—rarely—one can improve an adviser's day by being creative. When this happens the adviser will thank you and shake your hand and look grateful for the temporary boost.

It was not my fate to stir any atoms of humor in my present adviser. The fact that I was one and a half times older than the ordinary undergraduate didn't seem to register.

"Have a seat, son." He sounded like a recording. The most casual observation would enlighten even a microbe that I was three or four years older than the adviser. I sat down.

"What can I do for you?," he asked mechanically as he stared absently toward a dust-covered rubber plant in the corner. I looked at the rubber plant then back to the adviser, then back to the plant. I decided I'd wait for the plant to speak first.

"I was addressing you, sir!" It was a voice cultivated to savage young whippersnappers.

"Sorry, sir," I replied passively, "I thought you were addressing someone else." He placed both hands on the desk as if to spring at me, gave me his most beastly stare—which was marred some by a twitching eye—and snarled:

"And just *whom* did you suppose I might be talking to?" He emphasized this with an inclusive wave of the hand.

"Well, I hardly knew at the time, sir. I mean, it was confusing, me sitting over here and you talking to the plant over there in the corner."

His twitching eye began to oscillate faster and I could hear his teeth grinding. The stare he gave me was doubtless intended to vaporize my spleen. I smiled and stared back. I could have matched him stare for stare and we might have been there yet, but that throbbing eye of his was a little hard to take. He had an unfair advantage. So I winked at him. Immediately his eye stopped twitching, but his bushy mustache began to quiver violently. For a frightening moment I was afraid I *really* had a problem on my hands. I turned and looked vacantly out the window. Presently he said:

"It's, er, 'bout time for my coffee break. I think I'll let you work with Miss Williams."

Miss Williams was in her mid-thirties, unnecessarily spinsterish, and so thin I could see the blood trickle through her system. She sort of "perked" when her heart beat. It would take two or three of her size to cast a respectable shadow. She would be perfectly safe if lost in lion country. No lion would bother her—unless he needed a toothpick. She was uncommonly businesslike and perceptably uneasy.

"Let's see now, what do we have here?" She fidgeted with the papers and looked up:

"What had you planned to enroll in this semester?"

"Well, I hardly know," I replied. "I thought psychology sounded like fun."

"Fun?" She looked puzzled.

"Yes, interesting, anyway."

"Very good, sir. Now we're getting somewhere. What particular field or branch of psychology are you interested in?"

"Oh, I'm interested in abnormal psychology," I said.

"Splendid field! Very interesting. You should love it. I've had a few courses in abnormal psych," she said.

"That figures," I muttered.

"I beg your pardon?"

"I said what fingers—you have such lovely hands." She blushed. She didn't have to try hard. What little blood she had was near the surface anyway.

"Why, why thank you! That's very kind of you." She was a-twitter and gushy. She was not familiar with compliments. "What particular phase of abnormal psychology are you most interested in? Adults? Children? Animals?"

"Insects," I replied as casually as I could. There was a pause.

". . . Insects? . . . Abnormal psychology of *insects?"*

"That's correct."

She looked terribly perplexed. Hesitantly, she reached for the course catalog, and thumbing carefully through the psychology courses said:

"I'm afraid, sir, that we do not offer any courses in abnormal psychology of insects. Perhaps there is a course or two on the graduate level, but I'm almost certain we do not offer it in undergraduate studies." Closing the course book, she said, "In fact, I'm positive."

I looked hurt. "Surely you don't mean it. Can it be that a school of this magnitude, this dimension, this greatness, doesn't have a complete program in psychology? Why, I was certain a school of this nature, these proportions, this caliber, would be complete in every detail. You're absolutely certain about this?"

"Yes, sir, I'm afraid so."

"This is sad. Very sad. I so had my hopes set on that particular discipline. It is depressing." I sat staring gloomily into the corner.

"Well sir," she said, with a touch of compassion in her voice as she reached over and patted my hand in a motherly fashion, "possibly there is something else we could interest you in."

I looked up ever so grateful. "Do you think so?," I asked. "I mean, do you really suppose there might be *something,* some hope?" She squeezed my hand and I squeezed back.

"Oh, I'm certain we could find something that would hold your fascination!" She squeezed my hand harder, I hung on.

"Tell me," she said huskily, "isn't there *anything* here that interests you?" The pupils of her eyes were dancing like a cricket in a jar. She was leaning over the desk smiling, holding my hand in both of hers.

"Yes, there is something I've been wanting to do," I said, looking deep into her eyes.

"Yes, yes, go on!" she encouraged.

"I think conversational Swahili would be lots of fun!" She dropped my hand on the desk with a resounding thud, wiped her hands on her skirt, and said with immense sarcasm:

"That sounds fine, sir. Why don't you just step out to the desk in the lobby and fill out your schedule and we will see that somebody takes a look at it."

I thanked her for being so helpful and retired to the lobby where I filled out my schedule and by the word *instructor* initialed it D.I.M., which stands for Did It Myself.

Part of the adviser's job is to see that the student has the required courses and the correct number of hours to graduate. Ask any senior if he ever had a graduation check before his final semester. Nine of ten will inform you he did not. A graduation check insures the student that he is progressing toward a degree on a specified graduation date. An impressive number of seniors each year are required to enjoy yet another semester in school and pay room and board, tuition and fees, and other living expenses, while they sit through *one* class which some adviser overlooked. It does not endear those students to their alma mater. The fact is, *any* student who can make passing grades through his freshman year is capable of taking the course catalogue and a copy of the graduation requirements and working out his own schedule. Then, before the student enrolls for his senior year, he can have a graduation check run on his academic record and find *exactly* what he needs to graduate. If the student gets an indifferent adviser or one who hurries through the check he should come back in two days and have it checked again. And he should ask for a different adviser.

Just because I am not personally acquainted with any advisers who have a conscience does not mean *one* does not exist. Perhaps even a *few* are scattered here and there throughout the academic world. However, if they all got together at one party, I suspect they couldn't make enough noise to get evicted.

# 5

# Student Housing

One has not experienced unmitigated exasperation until he has conducted a search for decent housing in a college community. There are two directions to travel: the student can stay in a dormitory or other regimented facilities owned and operated by the school, or he can reside elsewhere. At most colleges and universities *elsewhere* is to be preferred.

Most school-owned housing is clean, neat, reasonably comfortable, and small. In all cases you may depend on it being small. These quarters may appear substantial in all respects when you see them standing empty in the summer. In fact they may look absolutely cavernous at that time. You walk around and your footsteps echo hollowly and dismally in the vastness of the place. You are told casually that you will, naturally, have roommates. Anywhere from one to three of them, depending on the size of the apartment or room. You nod absently because it does not occur to you just how much room four people and their baggage can take up.

Human nature being what it is, the first roommate will arrive three or four days early. He settles in, gets first choice of everything, and rattles around in the place with all the tranquility of a well fed sheep. A couple of days later, just about the time roommate number one is going stir-crazy, roommate number two shows up with his Volkswagen full of necessities. A few adjustments are made, and the apartment begins to take on a contented, homey atmosphere. Everything swings along peacefully until about nine o'clock of the evening before classes begin. Whereupon roommate number three arrives with his eight-year-old supervan crammed full of essentials, plus a ten-speed bike, a guitar, a variety of electrical equipment, a backyard barbeque outfit (a delightful addition to a ninth floor apartment) and his collection of assorted cookware. Things are rearranged to accommodate the new boarder and a feeling of uneasiness begins to permeate the air, as it is obvious to even the most casual observer that the apartment has shrunk alarmingly. It is adequately populated. It is already operating at full capacity. It is obese with humanity.

At ten minutes after one, the fourth and final roommate arrives in his Mercedes truck, pulling a rented trailer. War breaks out; peace treaties are made and broken; territorial rights are drawn up and violated; boundaries are established, and then dissolved; pandemonium, aggrevation, and perpetual irritation also move in for the duration.

The problems are monumental. What the hell do you do with four full stereo sets, seven speakers, three hundred LP albums, ninety tape cassettes, three ten-speed bicycles, two guitars, a full drum ensemble, a trumpet, a large art easel, fifty-six assorted pots and pans, thirty-two pairs of shoes, a remote control airplane with five-foot wingspan, two backpacks plus sleeping bags, a ham radio set and its equipment, two sets of golfclubs, some tennis rackets, a few frisbees, complete archery equipment, a pair of skis, and not least, a full-sized Honda which cannot be left outside for fear of theft. It also leaks oil.

When everything is safely inside, there is a pile roughly four feet high in the middle of the living room floor. It does not change substantially during the remainder of the semester. Actually, things went pretty well, which means that while there were local fistfights, there was no hitting below the belt.

But a good thing cannot be expected to last forever. At twenty minutes before eight the next morning, four obnoxious alarms went off within seconds of one another. The realization that everybody had an eight o'clock class every morning did not meet with unanimous approval. There was a frantic dash for the bathroom, the more alert and swift of foot having the advantage over those who lingered a moment too long. The vexations and frustrations of dorm life had settled upon campus inmates for another semester.

There are certain noticable advantages to living in a dormitory. On any given night it is not difficult to find others who are more interested in furthering their social life than their academic career. It is not impossible to locate a party or parties who are willing to order a pizza and split the cost, or to find enough people to play cards until two or three A.M. Perhaps the only thing harder than finding a quiet place to study is to find somebody to study *with*.

There are a few rules that one must pretend to abide by if he is to live harmoniously in a dorm. One of these is that no party is to play his stereo louder than five on the ten-point volume control. Actually anything above three-and-a-half relieves all residents of that floor from the worry of studying because it is impossible. But it is not for the resident's benefit that the volume control is enforced. There is a general and very real fear that any vibrations above seven-and-a-half might deteriorate the basic structure of the building.

At most colleges women living in school-owned buildings have to observe what are referred to as *hours*. We shall delve into this aspect of living in another chapter. Also, at most colleges, the rent is higher for school-owned living quarters. This is mostly caused by an ingenius and fiendish tax imposed by the school. We shall refer to it as a boarding tax. What it means is that your meals are included in your bill. Yes, contrary to general opinion, you do have a choice at most of these dining halls. You can eat what is prepared for the day or go hungry. That's the choice. The school has a logical explanation for this kind of folly: it very nobly states that the student is assured of having three well-balanced, nutritionally correct meals every day. I can state as an almost positive fact that not one severe case of rickets, or even scurvey, has been found among off-campus dwellers in the past forty years.

An off-campus apartment has several advantages, mostly social—provided you begin your search early enough to find decent accommodations. And by early I mean four to six months ahead. All really great apartments, those with fireplace, plush furnishings, etc., are booked for fall semester before kids leave for summer break. The next best lodgings, those neat garage apartments or garrets with that comfy scholarly feeling and a built-in bar, are reserved next. Then we get into the more mundane quarters: average, uninspiring, pedestrian-type housing. As summer progresses, these dwellings, too, are rented and the no-vacancy signs begin to go up. By August first, one must possess a keen eye in order to spot the few remaining "For Rent" signs near the campus. At this point an apartment is judged no longer on its furnishings but by the squish test. As soon as the door is opened, you dash into the darkened room and stamp fiercely once with each foot, then turn on the light and count the casualties. If you scored less than three roaches, take the apartment. You have found a desirable den. With work and dedication you can probably hold your own against the other residents. If your test fetches more than five specimens, and you decide to take the place anyway, rest assured you are going to be a part of the minority as long as you stay there. A word of caution is in order here. If you stomp on something and it squirms—leave. Do not turn on the light to observe your conquest, just leave. Whatever the victim, he has friends.

It is with no particular enthusiasm that I report my arrival—three days before school began. The local paper was full of listings for clean, neat, comfortable air-conditioned apartments. There were also listings for trailer houses. A trailer house has never been a comfortable abode; certainly not a trailer house designed for rental in a college community. If you own a brass monkey as a lawn ornament, he is just as safe outside on a winter night as inside the trailer. In the summer leave him outside by all means. A brass monkey, sitting in a trailer on a hot summer day, will get as mushy as a Hershey bar in the glove compartment of a car.

I do not jest when I say the first apartment I checked was a converted chicken house; converted by adding panes of glass over the screen windows, and introducing a bed, a rickety cane-bottom chair, and a washstand. The next place was some improvement but still it had a dirt floor. Another ad said: "Nice country residence, quiet, livable, six miles from town." True, it was only six miles from town—as the crow flies—but if the crow had to follow the road it was eleven miles. A pleasant old farmer greeted me and took me out back to a seedy-looking shack. A supply of contented hogs lay in the shade of the raised porch.

The farmer forced the dilapidated door open far enough for me to peek in.

"You kin just move 'at hay thar into 'at side room, thur, an' this'll make you a cozy little place fer th' winter. Me'n the wife lived here fer nigh on twenty-six year afore we built the other house, thur."

I was preparing a few choice words for him when I dropped a cigarette butt, intending to grind it out. However, it fell through a crack in the porch floor and into the ear of an unsuspecting hog. There was instantaneous mayhem. The hog was a large critter, and in his moment of revelation he bounded to his feet; his back protruded up through the floor. His agonizing squeal alerted his able companions that something was amiss and they too leaped to their feet, their backs rupturing the floor here and there in the most unexpected places. In a more or less unified herd they departed for a less hostile environment, taking a good part of the porch with them.

When I finally untangled myself from the wreckage, I confessed that I was not interested in the place at that time. I told the farmer that while it was peaceful and quiet enough, I was afraid it had too much *country* atmosphere for me.

Back in town, I contacted a real estate agent who had several listings. We got in his wobbly-wheeled pick-up and clattered to several different locations, all of which needed repainting before they could be condemned. Finally he took me to a nice-appearing stone house, quoted me a ruinous price, said I would love it, and pushed me in ahead of him. It was a commodious shelter of six or seven rooms. Two or three epochs ago it had been a splendid dwelling, I suppose. Of late, however, it had rather fallen to decay. A mouldering old fireplace was crumbling to ruin. From the ceiling hung a pitiful, rheumatic chandelier. Part of the supports were broken, and only one globe remained to shelter a long-burnt-out bulb, while another receptacle holding one bare 15 watt bulb served more or less to illuminate the center portion of the room. The varnish was peeling off what had once been beautiful panelled walls. A piece of faded green burlap that had seen better days was serving as a door for one room while the door to a nearby closet hung precariously by one rusty hinge. A three-legged table, which had suffered an amputation, stood against one dreary wall, with its companion, a bottomless chair with no back. Every now and then little avalanches of plaster descended to the floor to add to what appeared to be an evolving stalagmite. The windows had been artistically draped by a creative herd of energetic spiders. The exceptional collection of spiders, I reflected privately, was probably why there was a noticable absence of roaches. The real estate agent casually stated that the plasterers would be over to repair the ceiling any minute now. In fact he could not understand why they weren't there already. When he began to describe the merits of the place, my first urge was to kill him, but one must admire the kind of tenacity that allows a man to carry on so serenely in the face of disaster. It was a magnificent performance. He deserved a reward but I could not think of anything appropriate.

"Surely," I thought, "here is a man who already realizes he is destined to arrive in hell and proceeds with the tranquil attitude that nothing can further damage his reputation."

He continued with the serenity of a Christian, with four aces: "Would you care to see the rest of the house?" he asked.

"I wouldn't miss it for worlds," I said.

He shot me a sharp look that dissolved into a vapid smile which revealed his twelve-hundred dollar gold bridge. He reminded me of another gentleman I once knew—who sold used cars. He's dead now.

We proceeded toward the kitchen. As we passed through a narrow hallway, it was hard not to notice a steady stream of water a couple of feet wide flowing down the stairs and into the basement. Obviously he wasn't going to mention it, so I quietly called his attention to the leakage.

"Oh, that?" he said. "Now *isn't* that a cute little waterfall! I almost missed that, and I knew they were installing one—you see, when they're finished there's going to be a lovely little pond in the basement with lily pads and flowers and—and—" He could see this one wasn't going to float. "And *actually* the plumbers will be here any minute to fix that little trickle in the upstairs bathroom." He gave me that thousand dollar smile again.

In the kitchen he got his second wind. Pointing to a wall of appliances that looked like refugees from a head-on train wreck, he said:

"Latest in modern conveniences! Fully electric—except for the stove, of course." (It was a woodburner, with no lids, no grate, no door, and two of the four legs missing.) The rubber sealing had vanished from the refrigerator door also.

"Color coordinated, too," he continued. By color coordinated he must have been referring to the grease-stained appliances, which matched the oppressively smoked walls.

"And how many kitchens have you seen with a chopping block?" he asked, pointing to a massive, lopsided oak table that sagged from its own weight and was so grease-saturated it dripped. All these conveniences were uncommonly intriguing, but my complete and undivided attention was riveted on an exceedingly unusual but wonderfully fabricated hole in the far wall. I had never seen a hole constructed in such a casual manner. I walked over and stood in it:

"What's it for?" I asked.

"Oh, that, well . . . er," he began to falter. It's sad to see a man's faculties desert him when a masterpiece is in his grasp. But his intellect failed him for once and he had to resort to the truth: "One of the former residents drove his car through the wall one night last spring. Those bricklayers were supposed to be here today to repair that."

Obviously he had shown me his best merchandise, which was a disappointment.

Motor-mouth and I parted company at that stop. While I was crossing the street to get to my car, a sparkling new Plymouth convertible rolled up beside me:

"Say fella," a husky, Mae West-type voice said, "you lookin' for a place ta stay?" I had heard the approach before, but something about the tone left me vaguely unsure. I turned to stare into a pair of grey, overly-decorated eyes which belonged to a worldly middle-aged blonde. Her hair came from a bottle, which didn't bother me, nor did the miniskirt which exposed a pair of firm, well-tanned thighs. With a set of pearly, if rather horsey teeth, she was massaging a wad of gum the size of a golf ball.

"I asked ya if yer lookin' for a place ta live?" she repeated, none too patiently.

"Yes I am. Why, you have something in mind—?" What the hell, nothing ventured, nothing gained.

"Get in," she said.

Having a philosophy that says: never pass up an opportunity for adventure, I got in. We zipped off down the street as though we were in a hurry. We exchanged mundane pleasantries while I rechecked the well-shaped leg that operated the accelerator and carefully observed a light blue sweater that was being severely imposed upon to keep everything under control. Soon we arrived in front of a series of duplexes, triplexes, and single-unit apartments.

"I own these," she said. "They were left to me, and I have one vacancy left. It's out back."

"Be damned!" I thought, "it's really going to be an honest business deal?"

It really was an *honest* business deal. It wasn't much of a house. Its growth had been stunted somewhere in its youth; there were the bare necessities—stove, refrigerator, desk, table, two chairs, a small bookcase and a bed. The bed had more lumps than a third-rate prizefighter's face, but it was adequate. The rent was extravagant, but not ridiculous, so I took it for one semester. I considered a proposition for the rent but the old gal looked like she had received an abundance of propositions, and another conquest of the flesh wouldn't make her that much difference. What's the challenge when a girl has round heels?

That night I moved bag, baggage and boat from the motel to my new quarters. I was carrying a cumbersome box, with no particular handles, and not having much luck with it, when I tripped over something that had parked itself in the doorway. I distributed myself and the contents of the box all over the living room as I landed. I broke out my more picturesque language and lit a match to see what had happened. Whatever had disrupted my progress was going to be in for a warm time! I collected my various parts and struggled into a sitting position. There, sitting on the door sill, and looking as content as if he were on welfare, was the most enormous and massive tomcat I had ever seen. He was a tabby; golden, silky, yellow, with dark amber stripes trickling around here and there. A magnificent creature. He was in luck for I happen to be one of the few men who likes cats.

Cats are the only truly independent creatures in the world, man included. The cat has domesticated himself because he could see it beat tromping around in the woods on cold wet nights looking for a soggy field mouse. The cat is the *only* domestic animal that never had to work for a living. That is *not* a dumb animal. In many ways he resembles professors—but the cat is less boring.

"Come in . . . Thomas," I said. What better name for a tomcat?

"Make yourself at home. You're welcome as long as you behave, provided, of course, you're housebroke." He looked the place over, found a comfortable spot on the unmade bed, and went to sleep. I assumed that meant he was satisfied and had decided to stay. I was not aware, at the time, that he had brought his baggage with him—about a thousand fleas. I continued to move in while he slumbered.

There were no roaches. The landlady assured me she had contracted to have a company spray for such vermin. And while the quarters weren't elaborate, they were clean and livable. Sometime after midnight I banished the cat to one side of the bed and arranged myself in accordance with the topography of the mattress. No sooner was the light out than the festivities began. The patter of tiny scampering feet and the squeaks and chirps that suggest to one that he is not alone echoed throughout the house.

"Hey fella," I said, poking the cat in the ribs with a toe, "how 'bout earning your keep around here? Go in there and stomp a few mice, or make a compromise, or something. See if you can get them to modify the racket some so a guy can get to sleep." His best effort was a soft grumble and he got up and moved about a foot to find a softer spot. "Some help," I thought, "mice are burglarizing the place and I'm stuck with an indolent good-for-nothing tomcat."

Either I finally adjusted to the noise or the mice became tired and less active, for I had been asleep for sometime when I was awakened to the melodious crunch of little bones and realized that Thomas was entertaining the other residents. In fact one of them was his guest for a late night snack. I reflected in a drowsy, contented way that it was nice to hear them getting along so well together. I dozed off with a smile on my face. Thomas had another mouse for breakfast, and by nightfall the house was vacant—except for the cat and myself.

If the reader be a high school student and contemplating college, or if the reader is already in college, but a prisoner of dormitory life, I cannot recommend too forcefully a move to the campus suburbs; for it is an established fact that living in off-campus housing is eighteen or nineteen times more fun. If you are the parent of a college student, and your offspring has been wanting to move off-campus, why not let him? After all, he is only going to be young once. Let us not hold it against him that he is adventuresome, and full of life and curiosity. If the student has maintained decent grades and has managed to stay out of jail or avoid pregnancy this long, why not show him you trust him completely? Besides, if you're a mother, and bored now that the kids are gone, it'll give you something to sit up nights and worry about. And it's almost certain the kids wouldn't think of doing anything you didn't do at their age.

# 6
# Professors

In the beginning God made idiots—that was for practice. Then He began on the menagerie and labored along until finally He constructed the ass. Everyone could see He was then ready to create a professor, and He did.

It was a mistake. He could see it immediately. Someday He'll do away with professors just as He did away with the dinasaur, the pterodactyl and the neanderthal.

Except for an occasional deranged one, a professor is usually harmless enough—if not roused. He has all the markings of an intelligent creature, yet he can't be allowed to run free and disturb everybody with his crazy theories. It seems a shame to kill him; he's such a simple thing—and harmless. We should gather them all up and put them in compounds. We'll call these zoos universities so as not to hurt their feelings. That way they won't bother anybody but one another. And people can come and watch them and someday we'll discover what they do.

In his own environment the professor is a curiosity. The academic community surrounds itself with large and ponderous words designed to impress, though not necessarily to enlighten. By this guide they can tell who is educated. It has no meaningful correlation to intelligence. Some professors have theories that are completely ridiculous; then there are others who haven't become completely anything yet. As a separate branch of humanity, self-classified as *homo intellectus,* the professor suffers from a disease not entirely uncommon among his distant relative, man. It is the disease of almost never being wrong. It is noticable that the better a professor is, the more often he seems to admit he is wrong—or does not know—while the poor professor is never publicly wrong. These latter are the intellectual flunkeys who fill the gaps at colleges and universities where it is not possible to get competent instructors. This encompasses a large percentage of the denizens of academia.

Professors are blessed with a good supply of Neuro-Dimensionalism—meaning the space between one ear and that of the other ear. This space is considered valuable territory—by its owner. How grateful many of us would be if there was a little more substance and a little less space.

Give an aspiring professor a Ph.D. and tenure, and watch the transformation. With this new status he assumes he is an authority. He will take to the soapbox to profess on any subject whatsoever. Professors are never at a loss for an opinion.

Of all the things a professor holds dear, what do you suppose he holds in highest regard? What does he worship first? What does he sit up nights to be thankful for? His wife? No. His kids? No. His many degrees? No. His noble mind? Hardly. His salary? Not quite. The thing every professor desires most is *tenure.*

What, then, is tenure? Why is this item so valuable? When a professor acquires tenure it means come hell or change in politics, his job is secure. At least that is what it originally meant. Before tenure was established for the security of competent instructors, each gubernatorial election in a state saw a fresh crop of "professors" invade the state-owned colleges. Many of these "professors" did not even hold degrees, for these were political appointments. The state-owned institutions were ideal places for the newly-elected governor to deposit helpful incompetents who were considered too honest or too moral to function as politicians. Today, tenure is primarily a license to steal, or at best to take money under false pretense from the taxpayer's pocket.

Scholarly endeavors and professorial inclinations were considered honorable professions in the pretenure days and before politics began to use the academic community as a dumping ground. In those days a professorship was as honorable as being the president of a company, or a newspaper reporter, or a cobbler, or a bootlegger. He was a rung above congressmen and men of the cloth. It was a noble profession in those days. But once politics gets its hand in something, you can never expect it to be the same again.

In the days when politics had its grip on the academic reins, an instructor hardly had time to get his desk arranged before someone else showed up to take his place. But today you can't move an entrenched professor with anything less than dynamite.

Now that we know what a professor cherishes most, now that we know that he is secure as long as he shows up for most of his class schedule, and doesn't sleep on the job (or if he sleeps, is discreet and does not snore too loud)—what could possibly trouble him? Of recent years there has been an energetic push in most academic institutions to have their professors publish. Surprisingly to the average citizen, who supposes that a professor is full of knowledge—or other matter—getting something published is a frightening problem. Just because one is a professor does *not* mean he is a scholar, not by miles. Not by millenniums. A professor is one who instructs, or pretends to do so, but a scholar is one who knows what he is talking about. It grieves me to report that there are comparatively few scholars in the academic world.

So what do scholarly attributes have to do with publishing? In order to write, it is necessary, generally, to have something to say. And therein lies the rub, for while many professors are leagues ahead of competent novelists in the art of sentence structure and punctuation, they have nothing to say. When they dip into their barrel of knowledge all they find is the consolidated, coagulated remains of other professors' ideas. Many of them have never had an original idea of their own. They are only a composite of the professors who taught them. It takes effort, dedication, and sweat to be creative. *Most* professors would rather see blood than sweat. I know one professor who thinks Manual Labor is a Mexican.

Only about 10 percent of our professors ever get published. Think of it! Only one out of ten! It's depressing. It's discouraging. It's disgraceful! What do they publish? Books? Novels? Revolutionary theories? No, most academic publishing is done in obscure journals which are read by few and appreciated by fewer. Invariably these manuscripts are dry, boring treatises filled with ponderous words and constructed in a fashion to guarantee obstruction of any fact that might be trying to acquire freedom. By now many people, who held professors in high esteem, believe, in fact are sure, that I am making a gross and unjust overstatement. I assure you it is the other way around.

If one thinks professors are the cream of the crop, the pinnacle of intelligence, one must have a very low opinion of the rest of what is referred to as humanity. For example: I heard a discussion recently between two authors—authors who write— who sell. The discussion was about the ability of professors to write:

"How many Ph.D.'s can you name who are well-known authors?" said one.

The other party reflected a few moments and could only think of two. The first author could only think of two— the same two.

Granted, a few professors do publish. Mostly they publish textbooks. I defy any man, woman, or child to pick up a textbook and read it for entertainment. If you *are* entertained by textbooks, it would be wise to keep quiet about it, for it's easier to stay out than get out. Not long ago I read a book by a professor on the wit and wisdom of humor— it was the saddest thing I ever tried to struggle through.

What I've been trying to explain is that few professors are scholars, and not being scholars they have mostly second-hand information at their command. Thus they are not qualified to foster new, worthwhile ideas. But professors are hired presumably as scholars. They are conveniently mislabeled scholars. And unfortunately many (most) think of themselves as scholars. Thus they attempt to write.

It is pathetic to see a poor, simple, kindly old professor, in the autumn of his years, trot out *his book* that he has been working on for 37 years. He comes tottering into the room and gently lays this dusty old manuscript before you. The first ten chapters are yellow with age and, if you read them, horribly out of date. Yet he fondles the pages as delicately as if they were the original copy of the Declaration of Independence. Rapture covers his faded blue eyes as he reminisces about this wonderful work. The glories he heaps upon the effort, as you politely scan a few pages, make you wonder for a moment if he is talking about the same manuscript you are staring at.

Feeling that you have paid your token respect by glancing over a few paragraphs, you gently rearrange the manuscript and hand it back to him. As he stands there talking and hugging the manuscript to his breast and babbling about how he "just hopes he can live long enough to finish it," you realize that this is his life, what's left of it. This worthless old manuscript is his child, his dream, his last hope for recognition. His aspirations are all buried in this venerable tome. How do you tell him it's 400 pages too long already; that editors aren't publishing big volumes much anymore. How do you tell him his masterpiece is so dry it could blot up Lake Tahoe? Obviously you don't, if you're civilized, or pretend to be, for you know this dreary manuscript will never cross an editor's desk. Why? Even if it is finished, the author is too much in love with his work to send it to a publisher. Why . . . why, they might turn it *down*. Refuse it! The gall, the humiliation, the shame!—after all, what do those editors know! No, even if it is finished the author will never submit it. He will keep it and look at it occasionally and admire it and bask in the contentment that *he* knows it's a masterpiece and that here, in his ancient roll-top desk it is safe from the vile hands and blue pencil of those offensive publishers.

One professor, in the college of business at the southeastern university where I did a short stretch, was so bothered by the fact that he had been unsuccessful in the business world and had to retreat to the world of academics, that he manufactured his own success. The second day of class this professor told us he had been a vice president of Investors Diversified Services. As a photographer of executives, I had done business with IDS and was aware that vice presidents of a company of that magnitude are salaried in a bracket that reaches well over half-way toward six figures. And not only are they respectably paid, but such men are in great demand by countless other companies seeking exceptionally qualified executives—so, what the hell was this genius of finance doing as an assistant professor at a paltry $12,000 a year?

Things of this nature always bother me. They make me suspicious— and I do not like to suspect people. If a person is legit, I want to know it. If that person is a faker, why the information can always be useful. A quick letter to the director of personnel brought a negative reply: "Sorry, we have never heard of Mr. ________." I filed the letter. Things droned along for a time. Then he laid the heavy news on us that he had been a executive vice president of Eastman Kodak— he had been called in to help the company solve some particularly acute managerial problems. Knowing considerable about the organizational structure of the

Eastman Kodak Company, I was again trampled with doubts. A hasty letter confirmed my suspicions. This letter was placed in the file to keep the other one company.

With two weeks to go in the semester, I had seven of these little pieces of correspondence— and a rather well-founded C going in the class. With Xerox copies of the letters under my arm I paid a visit to the professor, in the privacy of his office. We had an interesting, if somewhat abbreviated, chat on grades, decorum, honesty, integrity, blackmail, exposure, risks, and things of that nature. Finally we reached a mutual compromise that, under the circumstances, was satisfactory to each of us. We compromised on an A for my final grade.

A friend of mine, majoring in English Education, was suffering through an intolerable class in "The History of Linguistics of the English Language." It was a mandatory class for students majoring in English, taught by a dull young liberal bent on making the course as difficult as possible. With his unusual talents for being uninteresting and obscure, he was having considerable success at making the class unendurable. Something had to give. As the generally dismal grades were returned from time to time, it became noticable that two of the girls, sitting on the front row and right under the young prof's fuzzy, cantilevered moustache, were gathering A's for efforts which, upon closer examination did not seem materially superior to the labors of others.

Some students redoubled their efforts to acquire some semblance of a grade. But anyone using his intelligence could see that these two girls had something going. My friend began to cultivate their friendship and presently discovered that these sweet, cooperative young ladies were practicing the oldest profession in the world— for a grade.

This was gratifying news because both girls were not only graduate students, but married and employed by the English Department as teaching aids. The professor was a securely married man with a house full of offspring. There are only two ways to get a grade out of such a circumstance. One is to make a superhuman effort, even in the face of unfathomably poor instructing, and hope to pull through with perhaps an A, but most probably a B, or play by the rules set down by that particular professor. In this case, by cheating, devious processes, and extracurricular activities.

Loaded with the necessary information, my friend arranged a nice little chat with the professor, and laid his cards on the table. But the young professor wouldn't play. He laughed and said:

"You're a fool for trying such a stupid and ridiculous stunt, Mr. ________. While I freely admit to the pleasantries of which you so generously accuse me, there is no way your can prove your statement." Suddenly his eyes narrowed and he shot the student a quick glance— "Unless you have, er, pictures?"

"No, I'm afraid not, professor," replied the student.

"Then you are a fool of colossal proportions." The professor grinned with evil satisfaction. "You have just succeeded in flunking my course, and I have a very good mind to turn you over to the administration and have you drummed out of school."

"I wouldn't do that if I were you," replied the student.

"Oh, and I suppose you have an *ace* up your sleeve," sneered the professor with a pious air.

"No, sir," replied the student, "a husband."

"What?" Visibly moved, the professor leaned slowly forward to get a better perspective of the forthcoming message. "What did you say?"

"Well, sir, Lagilda, the tall redhead . . . you will recall, perhaps, her husband? He plays for the Raiders. Well, sir, you can't believe what an insanely jealous man he is. He's already annihilated three men in their two years of marriage. Now what worries me, sir, is what if he should find out— or even suspect that you and his lovely wife—"

"Ah, yes . . . I see what you mean," said the slightly built, and thoughtful professor. "Perhaps I was a mite hasty there. By the way, please accept my humble apologies for referring to you as a fool. I see I have considerably underestimated you . . . yes . . . yes. I think something mutually satisfactory to both of us can be worked out. In fact, I'm sure of it." The transcript reads A.

There was one professor of journalism, a shabby, overstuffed oaf who, in order to impress the class with his vast ingeniousness and aggressive attitude, told the students at the beginning of the semester that he bounded out of bed at six-thirty every morning and wrote a thousand words. Being typically absent-minded, this account soon escaped him. The second week of class, needing something to impress the students and gain new respect, he informed them that he rose at five-thirty every morning and wrote two thousand words— for practice.

That statement brought questioning glances among the students, for some of them had been awake the week before and remembered the original lie.

The fifth week this professor stretched believability another notch and announced that he was up each morning at *four-thirty* and wrote three thousand words. Each time the professor magnified this deed he became more pious and peered down his beak at the poor students. The simpering old ass had foisted this falsehood on his classes for years. It was an ego trip for him, having never had anything published.

Unfortunately, there was a habitual reformer sitting in his class that semester, one of those nonreligious missionary types who thinks nobody's habits need reforming as much as the other man's; the type of person who is not content until he has reformed that aching soul to his satisfaction. That reformer was me.

I'm a patient man and tolerant of those who occasionally stray from the truth. I have empathy for the citizen who magnifies the truth, for I have improved the truth upon occasion myself. But even among liars there must be a point of resistance.

First, I anonymously hired two wake-up services to call the professor, one at four-thirty and another at five o'clock. This wasn't as successful as I had hoped. The second morning he scorched the ears of both those young ladies with a brand of asbestos profanity that would have shamed a Greek sailor, and threatened to sue the organization if they bothered him again. Thereafter it became necessary to hire a young lady who worked the night shift at a large local resident hotel to ring him out of bed every morning at four-thirty.

He changed his phone number. It didn't help. He got an unlisted number. I bribed a telephone employee. He asked for another number. It was no use. He refused to answer the phone. It must have damaged his mind, the way that phone rang. He had the calls traced— they could have come from any one of three hundred phones in the complex. It is difficult to comprehend the seraphic contentment it has given me just to know he sits up mornings to hate someone he doesn't even know.

A friend of mine whose writing is well published was having difficulty with an instructor in creative writing. Things started off well enough and my friend, let's call him Bill, received an A on his first two papers. It was about this time the instructor discovered that Bill wrote a monthly article for a national magazine; had authored three books which were selling reasonably well, and wrote a Sunday column for a string of medium-sized newspapers. Immediately Bill's grade dropped to a low C. It remained there for several efforts. Finally, not having the time to struggle along trying to satisfy this pathetic sloth, Bill plagiarized a well-written but obscure story from the celebrated Mark Twain. Imagine his surprise when he discovered Mark Twain also made C's in this class. At the top of the returned paper— next to the large C— was a note in blue pencil. It read, "A good idea; but lost in a slovenly mind." Imagine that! If Twain were alive he would have sent an army of capable arsonists to burn that professor's house.

Having overcome the initial surprise of this professor's gross jealousies and hostilities, my friend plagiarized yet another paper, and still another. William Faulkner got a C and poor old incompetent Hemingway got a D for his efforts. Thus enlightened, my friend returned to writing his own papers and gave up trying to please the decayed turnip who posed as a writing instructor.

Bill continued to get C's on his papers and continued to send them off and get them published. At the end of the semester he had received checks totaling approximately three times the professor's salary, not to mention a large royalty income from his books. Bill did not want to cause undue trouble. When classes were finished for the semester Bill walked into the professor's office for a small chat:

"You know and I know that the work I turned in this semester is worth more than the C you're planning to send in for my grade. May I suggest you reshuffle and deal again— otherwise I plan to entertain myself at your expense."

Not being very smart, certainly not smart enough to recognize a bright student, the old fossil cussed him soundly; did it with feeling too; told him he couldn't write a paper that would interest a tadpole; said he couldn't pass a writing class for a kindergarden, and that he was damn lucky to be getting the D that he did not deserve!

Bill thanked him for his constructive criticism, and meekly backed out of the office. The professor, perhaps, felt a slight twinge of conscience at treating an obviously capable student with this kind of insolence, yet he was probably outwardly happy that he had put the upstart cub in his place. Within the hour he had probably forgotten the incident. Thus it must have jolted his crusty gizzard somewhat the day he absently checked the dusty pigeonhole where the department filed his mail, and discovered a notice from the *Board of Academic Appeals*. The notice read: ". . . the student in protest is one William Snodgrass, a junior who had been in the professor's creative writing class the previous semester," etc., etc.

To be summoned before the academic appeals board, at most colleges, is not a professor's idea of a promotion. Something has gone astray. Either the student is a nut, and is bluffing for a grade, which can be easily determined, or the professor is in error somewhere. If the latter is true, there are questions to be answered. The head of the department, who, if feasible, must stand behind his instructor, wants to know what happened. Why is this student attacking the department? How did the professor come to get himself in this unenviable predicament? What kind of a student was this? If the kid deserved a better grade, why didn't the prof give it to him? If he didn't deserve a better grade— then why is he causing trouble? Then there is possibly a dean or even a vice president who wants to know why this student is so dissatisfied. No, to be called before the academic appeals board is not a jovial occasion. Fortunately for the poor or lazy or jealous professor, *most* students are even more frightened of the appeals board than is the professor.

Thus it was that this professor of creative writing found himself, on the appointed day, sitting none too patiently, and not so comfortably, in the small room which served as the appeals court. There were six jurors; three teachers and three students.

The writing professor felt nervously confident. He had sized up the panel of jurors and decided the teachers, two women and a man, would doubtless be on his side— protection within the profession; honor among thieves; that sort of loyalty. Yes, he could count on them. As for the students, one boy, one girl, and one flat-chested, long-haired, dirty-nailed creature of undetermined sex, well, he could bully and browbeat them to his way of thinking. He'd had so much practice over the years. Victory was his. He would make this reptile of a student rue the day he ever thought about taking a writing course!

At thirty seconds before the appeals board was due to open for business, in strode Mr. Snodgrass, dressed in a natty, dark, pin-striped, expensive-looking suit, twenty-dollar shirt, conservative tie, and briskly shined black alligator shoes. He was carrying a small leather letter-case in one hand and in the other— an opaque projector. He exuded the confidence of a Napoleon. Some of the professor's own crisp confidence was replaced by a grey raveled uneasiness. No student had a right to look like that.

Each case has a referee, who presently arrived and called the hearing to order. The charges were read, to wit: "Mr. William E. Snodgrass claims bias and jealousy on the part of Jed J. Turnip, professor of creative writing, as the reason he received a grade of lesser merit than he deserved. . . ."

"That is pretty strong language, Mr. Snodgrass," said the referee. "I trust you have some proof to back these claims?"

"Yes, sir," replied Bill Snodgrass as he rose and stepped forward. "I believe I can prove beyond reasonable doubt that Professor Turnip was— is— jealous of my humble success as a writer." While talking, Snodgrass adjusted the projector for operation and flashed a copy of a theme on the far wall.

"Here was my first effort for this class. You will notice the grade (A) and the favorable comments penciled in the upper left hand corner. Now, here are the next two papers— also with a satisfactory grade (A). At this point Mr. Turnip discovered that I had some reasonably successful books to my credit, that I write for a national magazine, and author a weekly column for a small chain of newspapers. You will notice the grades of these next four papers— C, D, C, and another C. May I also call your attention to the choice bits of sarcasm scribbled in the upper left corner of these papers? It was at this point," continued Snodgrass, "that it seemed futile to try and make a grade under such a hostile professor. Suspecting the source of the trouble, I plagiarized a short, obscure story from Mark Twain's works. Here is the story, as graded by Professor Turnip. You will notice the abundant use of the blue grading pencil and the various notes: poor punctuation; sloppy construction— and my favorite, 'a good idea but lost in a slovenly mind.' I like that, but," he turned to the professor, "Mark Twain would have burned you out. And sold tickets to the performance, were he alive today."

"Here," continued Snodgrass, "is a little story I stole from William Faulkner. The Turnip gave it a C."

The Turnip began to squirm. The blasphemies he had prepared to unload on this wooden-headed student now seemed to be rather insignificant. The immense pleasure he had received in making up those stories was swiftly dissolving into a sort of mild panic.

". . . And here we have a neat piece I swiped from Mr. Hemingway," Snodgrass was saying. "You will notice the mighty Hemingway gets a D in this vegetable's class. And here is another story I wrote for Turnip's class— you will note the D. And here is a copy of the check I received from __________ magazine for that article. Here we see another paper, and another C, and here we have a copy of the check verifying the sale of that story."

Leaving the projector, with the check for $600 overlapping the story with the large, luminous D reflecting on the far wall, Snodgrass walked over to the panel and with a helpless, palms-upward shrug, said, "I ask you, if these esteemed journalists and brilliant novelists could make no better than a C in Turnip's class, *how* can a poor humble student possibly hope to make a grade in the class?"

Snodgrass's transcript now reads: Creative Writing— A.

An economics professor, whose brand of economic philosophy happens to be in vogue at the present time, hides out at a major midwestern university. This man is an acquaintance of mine, as I am commissioned, from time to time, to photograph him. He is one of the really bright professors. I qualify that statement with the following reasoning: over the years this professor has managed to get his salary increased at a steady rate, and his workload continually reduced until now the struggling taxpayers of that fine state are privileged to pay him in excess of $50,000 a year. What is their return for this investment of their tax dollars? One would naturally expect a hard-working, driving, energetic teacher, turning out legions of bright, scholarly economics students. Not so. This brilliant mind has been at work, all right. At work creating a reduced teaching load for himself. He draws this noble salary for teaching *three hours a week!* Wait; that is not for the complete school year. No, that is only for the *fall semester!* The spring semester is reserved for his many speaking engagements. Well, you say, fine, he is representing the university. He is, in a sense, part of public relations. That is true. It is also true that he won't budge from his office for less than $1,500 per lecture. The university that pays his salary cannot even ask his advice without paying him a consultant fee. I am told the federal government pays him an annual retainer fee plus a per diem when his advice is desired. Needless to say, all his expenses are paid when he is called away from his office.

At the age of fifty-four, this professor manages to scratch out a living on approximately $120,000 a year.

This does not count royalties from several successful books that he researched and wrote on the taxpayers' time. Perhaps you think I am condemning the man for ramming his hand so deeply into the public's pocket. I certainly am not! I think it is admirable that a man can retire at such an early age (since he was 31) and feed so handsomely at the public trough! Let us envy him, for most of us would do the same if given the chance.

Is this professor, this genius of economics, this fountain of business knowledge, of such inestimable value to mankind? I was privileged to photograph the new chairman of the board of one of our nation's largest companies one day, and in passing conversation asked if he happened to know Dr. ________? A sad, faraway look came into his grey eyes and he sighed:

"Yes, we know Dr. ________. We know him very well. We hired him, on a consultant basis, some years ago." The sad look descended into a generally gloomy and downcast attitude. ". . . It took us months to straighten out the mess he left behind." After a few moments of reflecting, he added, "perhaps he's good enough on matters of international economic logistics, but from a practical, profit-making standpoint he is walking disaster!"

# 7

# Lecturers

A friend, Professor X, in his book, *This Beats Working For a Living,* employs among other sarcasms the phrase, "The Ph.D. has become a license to steal."

Not having acquired a Ph.D. or the desire to seek one, I have not read the fine print on one of these prized documents. But I suspect somewhere it also states that a doctorate gives the holder a license to bore, for few indeed are the professors who rise above a universal dullness. It would take a fair sized Texas spread to corral the legions of professors who can take a reasonably interesting subject and reduce it to insipid trivia.

Most professor's lectures are flat as ditchwater. I am personally acquainted with four professors who could put a bolt of lightning to sleep. I know professors who are so dull students go to sleep during the hour exams. One tries his best to hate a professor of this nature, but it is difficult to hold a grudge against a vacuum.

I have before me second-hand information concerning a stimulant manufacturing company which, as a publicity stunt, created a national contest to find the professor with the highest "sleep ratio" in his classes. Students responded with such enthusiasm and presented so many names that the contest had to be held at Wrigley Field in Chicago. There were so many entries that there was no space available for spectators, so it was decided that the professors had to lecture to their fellow contestants. Each contestant was given fifty minutes, the length of a class period. Then there was a ten minute break to count the sleeping, and wake them up for the next round.

The contest had to be canceled at the end of the third day. Engineers feared that the destructive force of the unified snoring might damage the foundation of the stadium. There is no way of knowing who would have eventually won, but observers report it was magnificent to watch those professors trying desperately to stay awake so that they would not be counted as a vote for the lecturer whose turn it was to inflict suffering on the masses.

Professors often use the term "quite obvious" to back up vapid statements which could never give rise to an argument in the first place.

At the beginning of each semester many professors try to gild themselves in a golden spray of words that leaves the student expecting a great deal of substance from the class. It would be better for the professor's reputation if he would keep dark and weather it out. Students come to class expecting little. If that is what they get, they are not disappointed. In order to assemble seventeen weeks of lectures most professors resort to a fancy accumulation of trivialities. Their lectures are crammed with details that serve no useful purpose. Many students realize they can use their time to better advantage— and snooze through lectures.

The most pathetic case is the professor who *thinks* he's Bob Hope or believes he is Dick Cavett. Occasionally visual aids are used to attempt to liven up a dying class. This seldom succeeds because classroom movies are prepared by the zombies who deliver those same dull lectures. But the hum-m-m-m of the projector is a mild relief from the drone of the professor's voice. Many professors are so dull that sitting through their lectures is more painful than doing time.

A professor who has no humor (and, sadly, most of them don't) should stay away from jokes in the classroom. Invariably his jokes misfire, to everyone's embarrassment, and damage, rather than improve the lecturer's image.

In a forestry class, at a northwestern university, the professor, who was excruciatingly dull, had to be absent for a few days to attend a funeral back East. It was supposed he was attending his own funeral, as anybody in class could testify that he had been dead for at least half a semester. A young, likable, aggressive graduate student was enlisted to teach the class during the professor's absence. The graduate student did such a spectacular job (considering his competition) that when the professor returned and began his insufferable lectures again, the class, as a group, stalked out. They marched to the office of the director of forestry studies and demanded to have their graduate student back— and they got him! I never did hear what happened to the professor, but I'm sure his position was most uncomfortable. He must have been the laughing-stock of the campus. Especially among his colleagues— though many of them must have laughed nervously, knowing in their own hearts that "but for the grace of God it could have been me."

Too many professors permit themselves to look seedy. They claim "theirs is an honorable profession," then proceed to dress in discards from the Salvation Army. Other professors seem to have their clothes tailored overseas— by Abdul the tentmaker, with shirts by Sodowski of Warsaw. Professors will wear the same clothes to class day after day and it makes one dread to get near them. Then there is the new breed, known as aca-libs (academic-liberals), who refrain from shaving until they are sufficiently haired over (as if this increases intelligence) and wear unironed grey cotton workshirts and grubby jeans. I am referring to young professors, not students. They wander to class late and shoeless; climb on top of the desk, sit crosslegged, and lecture or, in too many cases, tell the class, "this is a class with freedom, man, so do your thing. We'll talk about whatever you kids want to discuss." This type of professor is popular with the kids. He teaches little (besides revolution) and the kids learn less. Happy situation!

There are ways a professor can tell if his lectures are boring: when kids bring pillows to class, the lecture is boring; when a professor has to keep raising his voice to talk above the increased volume of snoring, the lecture is boring; when he sees kids shaking their watches to see if they are still running, the lecture is boring.

Nobody in this world has to be boring, least of all a college professor. The *only* reasons a professor is boring are because 1. he doesn't know his subject well enough, and 2. he never really found his own field interesting, because indifferent instructors like himself presented the material in a lethargic manner, and like him, their minds had caked together from years of grinding away. What these professors need is a new brain.

"But," a whimpering professor says, "how can *anybody* make a subject like ancient history come alive. It's *dead!*"

Baloney! Ancient history is full of amusing stories and exciting events. It's stuffed with brilliant men and abysmal fools. No, ancient history isn't dead, the professor who can't take that rich material and entertain a class for a semester must have a brain that has congealed into solid granite. I used ancient history only because most people think of that subject with the affection a hemorrhoid sufferer thinks of sandpaper.

Then, of course, there is the amoeba who says:

"But, I'm not in a humorous discipline like history— I'm in science."

Science, ah yes, science is the droll discipline. Nobody expects science to be interesting to anybody but a four-eyed bookworm. *Any* subject can be interesting. The doctors and nurses who extracted my appendix had a delightful time (at my expense). They enjoyed their work. They enjoyed it more than I did, notwithstanding the festivities were prepared in my honor. Did they do a poor job because they enjoyed their work? They did a fine job.

Then there is the instructor who says, "my subject isn't entertaining because I know it too well. It is no longer a challenge." This man is busy deceiving himself. He does not *really* know his subject well at all. For example, ten years ago I was convinced my knowledge in photography was supreme. I assumed it covered the earth, so to speak. At that time my prices ranged from about twelve dollars to about thirty-five. In those days I thought photography was a very serious business. Today I think photography is fun. It clicks along very well; things are always developing; I'm getting lots of exposure, and I enjoy framing people. I also get from $435 to $1,500 for a finished portrait now. The difference? I know my subject well enough now to laugh at it, to enjoy it. A professional or a professor does not know his subject until he can see the humor in it. Only then have you arrived.

One morning last semester, in a political science lecture that was dull to the point of being demoralizing, two students struck up a conversation. They mumbled and whispered along for a while, but when communications finally warmed up they began to talk louder. At first it wasn't too distracting, because there were some four hundred students in the lecture hall. But when they began telling jokes and laughing noisily the professor could no longer tolerate the competition. A wearisome lecturer will seldom stand for any humor in his class. It makes him look bad. So he walked to the edge of the platform and with immense sarcasm said:

"Would you two *gentlemen* please be quiet so that the rest of the class could hear the lecture?" (As if anyone in the whole room cared.)

The students, being decent respectable kids, as most students are, looked a little embarrassed and slouched in their seats. They had momentarily forgotten themselves in facing such sterility.

Seeing his advantage and taking a deranged delight in such situations, the professor felt it safe to degrade further these poor dunces— who had meant him no harm.

The professor was doing his best to be scathing, something he was better at than lecturing, when a young lady of considerable beauty stood up on the far side of the lecture hall and demanded attention:

"Dr. Ripoff!" she said in a loud voice.

The place got deathly quiet. Shocked, the professor turned slowly to face her. "How could I lose control of a good thing this quickly?" he was thinking. Who's this upstart who has defiled my finest hour?

"Yes?" he said.

"I would like to know who was talking," she said.

"Why?"

"Because whatever they have to say has to be more interesting than your stale lectures," she snapped.

"GET OUT!— Out of my class!"

"I'm sorry but I'm staying. This isn't *your* class, sir; it belongs to us, the students. We pay for the dubious pleasure of coming to this class, and we pay well. Our parents pay taxes to help support this school and, unfortunately, you and dreary professors like you."

"GET OUT!" The professor was trembling with rage.

"But, sir, this is the first time you've been interesting; the first sign of life we've seen from you. I would hate to miss. . . .," she said.

"LEAVE!"

"I think I'll stay. I want to see how long you can function without your crusty old notes."

"I'LL HAVE YOU REMOVED— Consider yourself expelled from college, young lady!"

"You do not have the authority to expell me, sir. As a matter of fact, I've been thinking of asking *you* to leave."

"WHAT?"

"You should be ashamed to inflict such cruel and unusual punishment on this captive audience. We have done you no harm. We didn't *ask* to be here. This is a mandatory class. Who gave *you* a license to bore people? Is it part of your academic background? Have you, as an outsider, no mercy on mankind?"

The class stood as one and applauded. The young lady quietly sat down and soon order was restored. The professor tried to make a go of it again, but he was defeated for the day. His heart wasn't in it (his mind never was). Presently he struck his colors. Class was dismissed.

In time of war, the nation should collect these dreary bores and ship them out to lecture to the enemy. The enemy wouldn't bother them at first, thinking them to be harmless, helpless creatures, and probably feeling appropriately sorry for them. The language barrier would be no problem, as few of them make sense anyway; the really atrocious ones, I mean. If one of these animated sleeping pills can put two-thirds of a class to sleep in fifty minutes, think of the devastation three thousand of them could wreak on a unsuspecting enemy in the first half hour! If we could get them amplified, I believe we could— however, it is doubtful the Geneva Convention would condone such war crimes.

Many are going to believe that I have been too harsh on professors in general; too severe, too sharp, unjust. I admit I warm to the subject like a Tangiers shopkeeper warms to an American tourist, yet I feel I have been fair in my appraisal. Most of the incidents I cite are from unfortunate personal observation or involvement. The rest were told to me by *good* professors. There *is* some resentment among good professors, because instructors are paid alike. Quality of instruction or ability is not considered when the pay checks are made out.

Take two professors: One is an excellent lecturer, researcher, and writer; a credit in every way to the university. The other one stays drunk a third of the time, gives a lousy lecture, dresses seedily, sometimes forgets to shave. Both have been teaching twenty years. One has twenty years of experience; the other has one year's experience twenty times. Both will draw about the same salary. Who can blame the good professor for complaining?

What is the ratio of good to bad professors? The ratio is about two bad professors to one average professor. Excellent professors are almost as rare as a sober poet. Only about one or two percent are masters of the art of instruction.

Most students who finish college encounter about forty-eight instructors. Ask any college graduate (professors included) to name the good instructors he had. Only the generous optimist will name more than three.

A few, who were aware I was writing this book, asked, "aren't you afraid of reprisals from your professors?" The answer is no. First, it is anonymous, and second, those professors who read it will only see the man in the office next door. And that is fine with me as long as the taxpayer knows the difference.

Economics is usually a dull subject, yet last semester I thoroughly enjoyed an econ class. I enjoyed it in spite of the fact it was a seven A.M. class. I had to get up day before yesterday and walk a mile in snow up to my— constitution.

The professor was a lean, hungry, hawklike fellow with a natty wardrobe and piercing grey eyes. At one time he had sported a great shock of curly hair of undetermined hue. Of late, however, it had taken on a salt and pepper appearance. The bulk of it had settled down around his ears like a fluffy nest harboring a brown, furry egg. He was covered with a thin veneer of authority that commanded respect— even from a reformer like me. Yet under that veneer were layers of desire, determination, dedication, sharp humor, ability to present material, and a sense of timing as to when a class was ready to push on to the next step. That is a rare quality in a professor; as rare as an honest politician. But even more rare, he had the humility to realize when he had pushed his students into a concept they were not ready for, and would retreat and begin again. He was, unlike most professors, not afraid to ask if anyone did not understand. If you did *not* comprehend, you had *better* speak up! Yes, other professors will ask if there are any questions. They do it with the inflection in their voices that it is time for the fools and matriculating village idiots to speak up. In actuality they are deathly afraid someone will ask a questions they cannot answer.

In my career as a sporadic student, I have never known a finer professor. He handles a difficult, potentially dry, subject with deft tact and superior control— and he is interesting. He makes the subject interesting! I cannot give his name because it would blow my cover (no, he is not a relative), but, sir, I salute you! There are others like him out there, scattered sparsely throughout the farflung academic communities. They know who they are. The students know who they are. We all appreciate them! We thank them. They're the ones who make it all worthwhile. They are the foundation of the education process. They carry the load for the loafers, the nesters, the ho-hum hokes. But for these few, who publish, lecture brilliantly, and are dedicated, education would fold.

But now let us examine the more common type of instructor: The professor I am about to describe is the aforementioned lecturer on political science. The textbook for his class was a 512-page tome that slogged through the history of our country's government. The petrified lectures were not taken from the same text, and the tests— well, nobody was ever sure just *where* the tests came from.

Every class period we filled volumes with notes. As weeks passed the notes piled higher and the reading assignments increased to a score of chapters, and still we had no test, no quiz, nothing to indicate our progress or our potential grade. Finally, at midsemester, a comprehensive test covering twenty-three chapters and twenty-seven hours of insufferable lectures was announced. The test was inflicted and grades were posted. There was a sufficiency of wailing and a proficiency of profanity, but all to no avail.

When the class met again, that miserable incompetent symbol of democracy belched his disdain for his students:

"I'm ashamed of this class. The average grade was forty-three out of a possible hundred. You kids do not know *how* to study. And you cannot hope to pass this class with that kind of effort."

As much as I hated that instructor, I had to feel sorry for him that day. If the urge to kill and the opportunity to kill had coincided at that moment, I would have been the only one of those 419 inmates who would have escaped the chair.

That insignificant fool, who had allowed his brain to fossilize from disuse, realized vaguely that the students were not at fault; that they were a bright group, capable of grasping any reasonable theory or discussion. He knew the *real* reason the grades were so low was because the instruction was abominable. I know he knew, because I had written him a scathing letter telling him so. Still, he had to lay the blame on *someone,* and he wasn't big enough to take the blame, or man enough to admit that he and his slovenly approach to teaching were at fault. He did nothing to correct the problem during the rest of the semester. The final test was just as pathetic as the midterm exam.

If the professor knew he was a lousy teacher, then *why* didn't he do something about it? Reason: he didn't know *how* to correct the problem. He had been in a rut so long he didn't know how to get out. For all purposes the man is dead. He has ceased to function as a thinking, creative being. And for that reason I feel sorry for him.

# 8

# Running the Course

Each particular field of study has its own quirks, and the instructors in each field have their own ways of tormenting students. If the political scientist in the preceding chapter was merely dull, that might have been because dullness is a way of life among that species. Other fields encourage professors to be obscure, or trivial, or cranky, or freakish. To sort them out, I have written a student's guide to the various disciplines, all in alphabetical order.

*Accounting:* Accountants are the most wonderfully narrow-minded people in the world. Their whole life is confined to a column of figures barely half an inch wide. Nothing exists outside that column. Nothing external is tolerated within those narrow confines. Accountants are the only people I know who are more interested in numbers than in figures.

*Advertising:* I considered enrolling in advertising. I believe that anybody who writes copy like: "I cannot *contain* myself any longer to write you about how wonderful __________ is," needs all the help he can get.

*Agriculture:* State-owned land-grant colleges are a curiosity in every way. Especially in the Southwest animal husbandry—ranching— is a way of life. Many of the kids come to school in broad-brimmed, high-crowned Stetson hats, jeans, western-cut clothes, and driving a fancy new pick-up truck. They may appear to emerge from the country, because that's where they're from. Those kids may talk with a drawl longer than a dirt road and slower than cold molasses, but don't let that fool you. They *own* the country out where they come from. Miles and miles of it, as far as you can see. And it's level ground out there, too.

They're bright kids, smart kids. Their parents are in big business, the business of raising the beef and pork and vegetables and grain and produce for this hungry land of ours. It is a tough business. The capital outlay is fantastic, the cost of production is prohibitive and the profits are, most years, nothing to brag about. Some years crops are good and livestock prices are high. But many years there is drought, or insects infest the crops, or hail beats a crop into the ground in minutes. It costs just as much to grow that destroyed crop as it did the year the crops were good.

After my tirade on professors, why am I defending agriculture, especially when meat and produce prices are already so high? Because I'm afraid that thirty years from now, if nobody stays out there to improve production, I'll go to the store and find beef prices at twenty dollars a pound instead of two dollars, and tomatoes at five dollars a pound instead of fifty cents.

Besides, the kid from the country is different, sort of. He is scorned by the city kids. They don't realize that the boy with the big hat, wide belt with large silver buckle, and the rough-out boots is going back home in four years or less to run a place that is worth more than 90 percent of the company presidents in this nation could scrape together. The city kid who has to share a campus with the hayseeds might do well to remember that the funny looking "Aggie" can probably buy and sell a thousand city kids— and their parents. Yes, they're different. I've been to school with "Aggies." They're comical in their dress; sometimes crude in their manners; but remember, my city friend, what we pay for groceries depends on how well they are taking care of things down on the farm.

Incidentally, one midwestern university's college of agriculture staff was very upset when it heard the school had purchased an artificial turf for the football field. This looked bad for the land-grant image. An emergency council was held and money deployed for special research. Soon the Agri-Sciences department was hard at work developing an artificial fertilizer to put on the field. Irrigation specialists were searching for a way to distill artificial water to keep the field in proper condition. Biology was trying to create substitute aphids for the grass, while agriculture engineering was busy constructing a lawnmower for nongrowing grass. The agronomy department was going crazy trying to make that grass grow. They were also trying to improve the protein content. Animal husbandry acquired federal grants to breed an artificial goat to graze the area. What departments won't do to acquire more grant money!

*Agronomy:* Two courses listed are: "soil fertility" and "plant breeding." Is nothing sacred from the prying eyes of a nosy professor? Checking on the results is one thing, but arranging marriages between plants seems like we're sticking our educated necks in where we're doubtless not appreciated! Besides, crossing a shade tree with the onion is in bad taste— socially.

*Animal Sciences:* Here are some courses listed:

Carcass evaluation: There is a rumor that one major agriculture college tried to hire Joe Namath to instruct this class, figuring that few men had inspected more carcasses than ole' Joe. I wonder if they tried to contact Liz Taylor?

Poultry Breeding: Didn't the birds and the bees start the whole thing?

Egg production and hatchability: Seriously now, would you get excited about meeting a henpecked guy who gets his kicks out of hatching chickens?

I used to take young ladies out near the poultry barns for nocturnal activities. Our visits were rather frequent and finally one particularly dark night a poultry professor or perhaps a kinder title— professor of poultry— knocked gently on the side of the car and politely asked us not to roost out there anymore. He complained that egg production was falling off. He said the hens crowded around the windows and tried to see what was going on, so would we mind parking elsewhere? We didn't believe him, but he was nice and so we moved on down the road and parked near the rabbit hutches.

*Architecture:*

Shelter design: elementary class, consisting of roof thatching and constructing and pouring of foundations for tree houses.

Acoustics, vibrations and noise control: This sounds like a noble class filled with volumes of practical information. After one resides for a few months in an apartment complex with wafer-thin walls, it makes one wish the class were mandatory for all graduating architecture majors.

*Art:* Of all the disciplines that are misrepresented to the student, art must be the most gravely misrepresented. The inference is that when a student enrolls in art school, he will be molded into a qualified artist, an artist capable of going forth, upon graduation, and making a living. This defies reason. Not one art graduate in five hundred could support himself, much less a family, on the sale of his art. The gifted artist, the one whose efforts are in demand, is too busy to teach. That leaves only the artistically handicapped to instruct.

When a chimpanzee can win first prize in national competition (as has happened) it does not leave me with the hots for modern art. When an expensive painting hangs upside-down for months in a major gallery and nobody notices the difference— or cares— it does not warm me to modern art.

Now, the offended legions of alleged artists will accuse me of being an ignoramus. Perhaps, but one year I painted 179 canvasses. Every one was sold before I began. Each painting was a copy of an old master or modern one. Yes, I know something about art. I have made some bucks as an artist. Not a respectable living, but I was paid what the work was worth.

In the days when art was respected, a master would take a few exceptionally gifted students and simply guide them in their labors. I use the word *guide* because a gifted student, who is willing to work hard, does not need a great deal of attention. What he needs is someone to keep him from making the small mistakes. A gifted artist has overcome the worst difficulties by the age of ten.

Good advice to the prospective artist: If you are not exceptionally gifted at freehand drawing when you enter college, it would be best for you seriously to consider painting houses and barns, or sawing wood, for you will need a means of support for your art. Of course, you *could* teach, but it is better to stay honest.

*Astronomy:* Being a reminiscing sort of fool, I recall the time I was commissioned to photograph a series of "regent's professors" for a large northern university. One of these gentlemen, a thin, rangy lad of seventy, with a disheveled shock of white hair holding down an angular face that harbored a twinkling pair of faded grey eyes, was a professor of astronomy. He was a dutchman by the name of Wyllum Luyten, and one of the world's authorities on the small white dwarf stars. A more sociable or likable fellow I never met. We had a delightful time working together. I asked many foolish and, I'm sure, childish questions about astronomy. Finally he asked (as if he didn't know):

"Just how much do you know about astronomy?"

"I understand what a light-year is. Other than that— virtually nothing."

"Fine!" he said.

"I don't understand," I countered.

"I only wanted to know the extent of your ignorance," he said, as his eyes twinkled, "so that I could talk on your level. Now, would you like to know something about astronomy in general and the dwarfs in particular— or is your palaver only to draw out my reactions so that you can photograph me in character?"

"Both," I grinned. "First I have a professional obligation, which you understand. Second, I *am* interested in what I can learn from you in the time that we have."

We spent about two and a half hours together and he instructed me the whole time. That was several years ago. I do not know whether Professor Luyten is still living and enjoying good health. I hope he is as active and dedicated and pleasant as when I had the pleasure of working with him, for he is one of the truly great ones. I shall always envy his capacity to enjoy life and his ability to transmit that quality to others.

*Botany:*

Plant anatomy: Sounds like fun. I wouldn't mind checking under a leaf or two, and studying limbs has always been a favorite pastime. Checking out a few tomatoes wouldn't be so bad, either.

*Chemistry:* Understanding chemistry well enough to make a

grade is one thing, understanding it well enough to teach it is a nag of a different hue. Doubtless three-fourths of the lower and middle levels of chemistry are wretchedly instructed. There are two reasons for this: many times the courses are taught by graduate assistants who are too involved in their own studies to have time to prepare to teach their classes properly. Absurdly low-quality instructing results when a professor who has attained some degree of renown in his field is forced to teach a sophomore or junior-level course. Invariably the instructor feels superior to such mundane "kindergarten studies" or "baby biochemistry" as one professor, with an elevated opinion of himself, called a class. This kind of professor shows his disdain by looking down on students, giving impossibly hard tests, teaching on a level far above the class's ability to comprehend, and making students feel insecure when they ask questions.

How much better it would be, how much more it would be appreciated, if the instructor would use his superior knowledge to present the material in a simple, complete, understandable manner, making sure each point was thoroughly explained and understood before moving on to the next one. An educated fool is of no value in the classroom. It takes *intelligence* to prepare and teach a difficult subject so that it is interesting.

*Civil engineering:* In any school noted for its advanced standing in the various fields of engineering, there is one department that stands supreme, civil engineering. At one rather average school of engineering, civil engineering has 350 hours listed. Sixty-eight of these hours overlap architectural engineering and could be taught together to save time, money, and manpower. Yet because of professional pettiness, it would be impossible for the two departments to agree on course content or class schedules. Thirteen hours could easily be saved by sending the civil engineering students over to the school of geology or vice versa. Yet again we have differences which exist more in the mind than in reality. Petty department jealousies keep these combination classes from existing. Fifteen hours could be as easily acquired in the department of chemistry at a considerable saving to the college. That is, a total of ninety-six hours of teaching per week could be saved. That would save about twelve yearly salaries, or well over a hundred thousand dollars in either taxpayers' money or, if it be a private school, donations from private citizens. When you consider that most college departments are about equally overstaffed, it tires the mind— and the pocketbook— to think about it.

*Clothing, textiles and merchandising:* I once took a course in fashion merchandising. It seemed like a good place to meet girls. I can highly recommend it for that purpose. That particular school considers itself (and is considered) as one of the better ones in CT&M. This has always been a curiosity to me. The school is located not an inch closer than 1,300 miles from the nearest fashion center. The head of the department, whom I know better than I would prefer, has never worked in the garment district, has never labored in any of the fashion centers of the world, has never created an origional design that was accepted— or stolen— by any design house, nor done anything not associated with a textbook or the classroom. Yet she is a self-ordained authority on fashion. It is curious, because she wears her hair the same as she did twenty years ago. She wears shoes that were stylish before my grandmother's time and her dresses have been the same length (about four inches below the knee) for the past ten years.

One cannot help but admire this old maid. Think of the handicaps she has overcome to be a fashion authority!

Costume design: This class, to instruct students on the future designs of clothes, is taught by a *much* more conservative dummy than the head of the department. This unmarried specimen sports a hair style which sweeps back into a comely knot at the base of the skull. Her face is decorated with an arched nose, which slants somewhat off the perpendicular, and, by prying, manages to separate two narrow, beady, nervous eyes. Strangling a skinny neck is a tightly buttoned high collar of the habit type. Full length sleeves sweep down to talon-like hands. White, spindly legs disappear into ample-sized shoes made on the same last as were my combat boots. This is the inspiring matron who teaches aspiring students in the design of future clothes. Perhaps her day will come— again.

My collection of assorted friends from those days includes twenty-three girls who graduated with a degree in clothing, textiles and merchandising. Some are now housewives, a few are secretaries, one checks groceries, one runs a day-nursery, one is a lady of the evening, and one works in a dogfood factory. The closest any of them ever came to getting a job in her field was when one of the girls modelled swimsuits. Like many college fields, the output of graduates exceeds the industry's demand.

Fashion merchandising and problems in fashion store management: This class is taught by a lady who has never worked in a managerial capacity in a fashion department and certainly has never been responsible for purchasing or merchandising. Like so many professors, she is stuffed with textbook knowledge and theories.

*Computer programming technology:* lists two classes in accounting (eight hours) that could be just as easily included in the accounting department's program.

*Construction technology:* There are fifty-five hours of construction tech classes listed in one college catalog. Thirteen of these hours could be better allocated to particular classes in the school of architecture. And nineteen hours are identical, in catalog presentation, to courses offered over in the civil engineering department. One class, a three-hour course on a senior level, called "A History of Construction," must have been created to afford employment for someone's relative. It is hard to imagine *seniors* needing a course in the history of that field. The course is mandatory for all seniors in that discipline. Translated that means someone is padding his department in order to secure more money.

*Drafting:* This course of study has nothing to do with the army. Drafting is the skillful and accurate drawing of new parts or plans and layouts of machinery and such related engineering subjects.

One drafting instructor called roll the first day of class, then said:

"Here is a syllabus of your class projects and assignments. Your textbook will cover any technical problems you might have. The dates are listed in the syllabus as to when each assignment is due. Turn in the completed assignments to me. For the duration of the semester I can be found in my office, room twenty-eight, building 219. You may begin at your leisure. Good luck." He walked out and was not seen in the classroom again. If ever a man drew money under false pretenses this must be a shining example!

*Economics:* With the exception of a scarce handful of individuals in business or government, economics is a discipline which survives upon itself. By that I mean economists either teach economics, or bus dishes. The market for economists, outside teaching, is *very* limited. Perhaps the following little story gives some insight as to why big business does not want to hinder progress with a staff of economists:

In a class of economic problems, the professor had warmed to his subject and was relating one hypothetical incident after another. Each incident was solved with a new economic theory. Finally, not being able to stand it any longer, one of the brighter students said:

"But, sir, these are all hypothetical problems. There isn't *one* practical problem in the whole lot."

The professor stared at him in disbelief for a moment, and then said:

"Economics is theory. It has nothing to do with reality. It does not concern itself with fact."

Of course that is not the real statement, problem, or condition of the study of economics. But that professor's statement has received more damaging publicity against the discipline than hundreds of hours of lectures have done *for* it.

For the sake of qualified instruction, economics should be limited to not more than a dozen universities in the nation. At the school where I am presently an inmate, the department of economics offers 203 hours. How many hours are necessary at a school of this size? Less than half would be adequate. But the head of the department is an aggressive, devious, and capable man and he has padded his department very well.

*Education:* Next to art, the various schools of education and the untold numbers of small teacher's colleges are presently doing students the greatest injustice.

I say presently, because there was a time when our elementary and secondary schools were in desperate need of teachers. Today teachers are surplus. There are about forty applications for every teaching vacancy. Fortunately, *good* teachers are still in great demand at all levels of education. If you're a taxpayer and you have kids in the public school system, or plan to have kids in the system, or have had kids in school, you must have wondered about the quality of teaching in the system. My father has been teaching in the public high schools for over thirty years. I believe it can be said, without straining something, that he is one of the good ones. Yet in over thirty years, he says, not one administrator has ever set foot in his room to see if he was teaching or sleeping. In short, nobody cares whether your kids are getting an education or not. Nobody but you and those teachers who want to see a kid get an honest chance in life. Too many teachers just don't care— except on payday.

Why do they have such a careless attitude? Much of it stems from what they observe in college. An aspiring teacher goes to college four years to become qualified to teach. What do they find at college? Incompetence mostly. Instructors who are poorly dressed, so they make a note of that; instructors who do not prepare for their classes, so the student makes a note of that too; instructors who give dull lectures; and instructors who practice doing as little as possible. This is the predominant college scene. Supposedly, these people are at the top of the educational heap. It stands to reason, then, that if one is to teach in high school or elementary school it is only necessary to put out about half as much effort as these practiced, professional loafers who teach maybe as much as twelve hours a week! This does not inspire even the potentially good teachers to extra effort.

Then there is the common practice of hiring professors who know as little as possible about their subject, the less the better, if would seem. Now, scholastically a professor may be a whiz. He may have a doctorate in his specialty and therein lies the rub. These professors, in their quest for a Ph.D., have stuffed themselves so full of theories they can hardly walk. Theories are fine. Theories are necessary. But theories, unproven theories, without practical experience, must be viewed with some caution. Most teachers who are teaching students how to be teachers have never held a job in a public school. Think about it. Ninety-nine percent of those who instruct in the art of elementary teaching have never taught in an elementary school. The man who created the modern concept of the "open school" for the lower grades, never taught in an elementary situation. I am not saying the concept is bad. I am only saying, let us not count the votes until all the returns are in.

Student teaching is part of the curriculum of every student proposing to teach in a public school. This consists of going out and observing a competent teacher for six weeks as he conducts daily classes. A student teacher is expected, reasonably enough, to teach some during the six-week period. All too often this time turns into a dreary sentence of being forced to sit in the back of the classroom and listen day after day. Or to be a captive slave for the teacher, who has the student teacher do all the grading of papers or standing hall duty or playground duty.

It is during this student teaching period that many future teachers discover that what they want least is to become a teacher. They find out that many of those great theory classes on child psychology and adolescent behavior are as perforated as Swiss cheese. They discover that most of what they have been taught does not apply in the classroom. This is a satisfactory way to send out many very bitter young teachers; teachers who feel they do not owe anyone an education because nobody saw to it that *they* were educated, but only given a degree, a license to steal from the public.

The student-teaching requirements do not usually come until the last half of the third year, or the first half of the last year. Many students feel this is too late. One young lady, sitting in an adolescent-psychology class, was vehemently criticizing the educational system. She had just returned from her student teaching and found that teaching was not her bag.

"But," she said, "I only have so much money to spend on an education. And here I am almost ready to graduate. I am now *forced* to become a teacher. I can't afford to be anything else at this late stage. Why couldn't I have done my student teaching, or at least a couple of weeks of classroom observation, when I was a sophomore? Then I could have changed my major in time. Now I'm stuck!"

She was unhappy. She is not alone. How would you like for your child to be in her room for one year?

As for school administrators, a substantial percent are coaches who didn't make it as successful leaders on the field. So they went back to school and acquired a master's degree in school administration and became principals or superintendents.

*Educational psychology:* In theory, educational psychology could be a wonderful aid to the beginning teacher. The psychological reasons as to why a child behaves as he does, or how to deal with a child whose parents recently got a divorce, would be of great help. There are *many* ways in which psychology if applied *practically* could benefit all levels of education. Instead, the study is infiltrated with theorists who have never taught in a public school. The only time they have contact with young adults is when they are conducting pseudo-research. Their idea of a child's behavior pattern is derived from observing rats. If the child runs the maze faster than the rat, then the information is studied and fed into a computer and compared to other statistical data, and it is finally ascertained that the child may or may not be smarter than the rat. The final outcome would depend upon many factors— the size of the room in which the test was given, the color of the walls, the time of day, whether the light was tungsten or fluorescent, and whether the child had his tonsils removed. Had the rat had *its* tonsils removed, etc., etc. These walking oxymorons get so bogged down in unnecessary variables that they can never make a worthwhile discovery.

The great abilities of the Ed. Psych professors lies in their enthusiasm for new tests for students to take— measuring learning experiences, they call it. Unfortunately, not one of these tests can tell a new teacher what to do when a kid, spaced out on drugs, disputes an issue with a long-bladed knife. Not one of those tests advises a teacher what to do about the girl sitting in the front row; she made top grades until three weeks before, when she found out her mother was having an affair. Nothing in the studies of Ed. Psych tell one how to analyze the problem of the girl who is scared to death she is pregnant.

Educational psychology could be helpful if its practitioners would refrain from giving tests to see how high a six-year-old can stack two-inch blocks in twenty seconds. What the classroom teacher needs is practical information; things he can apply to his everyday problems. The educational psychology departments with which I am familiar are ill prepared to deal with the facts of life in the classroom.

Those who perpetuate the discipline known as educational psychology are not content to be merely unhelpful; they work at being difficult to understand. From last semester's class I present this example:

"No principle in educational psychology is better established than, perhaps, the general idea that individualized attitudes depend on the perceived attitudes of significant others."

If that is one of their better-established principles— whatever it means— then let us encourage them to retire to the asylum. It gives me the vapors to try and analyze that sentence.

*Engineering:* I once had a roommate who was an engineering student. He stayed around that university seven years trying to chisel out a degree. He finally got it. I was always sorry for that. He would have made a better writer; I never knew a funnier person.

The slide rule, as most of you know, is the single most necessary item an engineer can possess— a slide rule and a large quantity of caffein tablets. I know of no discipline that foists more work on its students. The slide rule is a delicate instrument. If in proper adjustment, and in synchronization with the mind, it will calculate to one ten-thousandth. If the slide rule is not in proper alignment, a poor engineer can work forever and not get the correct answer. My roommate used his to swat flies, and sometimes he used it to prop up the window. Once I came in and he was using it to stir paint. And you wonder why it took him seven years to pry a degree out of that university?

Engineering is not my field, so its faculty is going to be allowed to escape. However, there is one story I shall relate:

I had been commissioned to do some Regent's Professors' portraits for a large Eastern university. This work kept me on campus for several days. Each day I walked to the library where I had been given a room to conduct my serial robbery. My route led me past an imposing building labeled Creative Engineering. I would probably never have noticed the building, except that out on the front lawn was a newly constructed canoe— constructed from cement. I presume anybody who is still warm could fine some humor in a cement canoe. Curiosity overcame me on the third day and I stepped in to ask about the cement canoe:

"Yes, we've constructed it."

"Will it float?"

"Certainly!"

"Well, er, is there a market for cement canoes?"

"Probably not."

"Then what's it for?"

"You see, sir, we've been challenged by another school's engineering department to a cement canoe race."

"Really? Who challenged you— the University of Warsaw?"

It turned out that they had been challenged by another large Eastern university. Both schools are highly regarded as engineering schools. Results of the race? It was almost a draw to the bottom. A site was chosen, a date was set. When the canoes were launched one sunk immediately but the other one beat it to the bottom. Bet the taxpayers of that Eastern seaboard state are delighted to hear about such concrete achievements.

*English:* It is difficult for me to write about the English department— *any* English department— and be calm. When I think about how many times I've been enrolled in English— enrolled with the intent to major in the discipline— it amazes me that I haven't burned out more professors than my records show.

I presume that nobody has ever attended a college and escaped freshman English. And that is only right and proper. Every one should be afflicted with this course. Those majoring in agriculture, engineering, and psychology have enough trouble writing so that people in their own profession can understand them. Let us at least instill in them the basic fundamentals of grammar.

Once a student enrolls in an English course more advanced than freshman composition, the atrocities begin. But first I must explain:

The idea of English as a discipline is noble. The purpose is to acquire a better understanding of the language and a competence in writing it. English is merely a precise form of communication. With this worthy goal, English has attracted some noble minds and superior intellects. Because the basic idea of English is to communicate, it is natural that the discipline has, over the years, attracted thousands of potential authors. Yet how many authors have a degree in English? I mean authors who have published books that have sold well. I cannot recall half a dozen. Yes, English professors have done textbooks, but that is a captive audience. How many professors of English have written books that sold, say, 50,000 copies? You could count them on your fingers and not crowd the digits.

Is there a reason for this lack of competent writers within the field? Certainly. Any writer with creative ability has sense enough to see what has happened to his professors of English. He can see that nobody could survive the curriculum set by English departments and remain creative. Why? Because the study toward a degree in English distills all the creativity out of a student. A graduate in English is a perfect stereotype. He càn spout laws of grammar to you all day. He can quote the parts of speech, and recognize them without flaw. He can take a difficult compound sentence and diagram it with ease. He càn write sentences that are fantastic for their perfect construction. His problem is, who cares?

English professors are probably the most insecure of all the geldings on any campus. Why? Every one of them wanted to be a writer, or at least to write successfully. Yet they end up instructing. Professing in English is a cop-out. It signifies, "here is another writer who never got off the ground." The faculty has provided for itself a neat shield from those who poke an accusing finger and say, "you're in English. You should be a great writer." The professor peers from behind a stack of books, looking all pious and innocent, and says, "I'm in literature. I'm a scholar in the great works of literary art." Then he drags out Shakespeare, who hasn't had a rest in three hundred years, and holds him up as the greatest of all writers; Shakespeare and his antequated phraseology. Hear them screech? I have needled dozens of English professors by blaspheming Shakespeare. Old Bill Shakespeare is far more dear to an English professor than God.

"So why don't you update the language in his plays?" I asked.

"Why, why— that would be a sacrilege!" they gasp.

"Why so? Is it because Shakespeare's works can't stand the strain of modernization?"

"*Certainly* they can!" they retaliate. "They are not modernized because we must keep them *pure*. It would damage the beauty of his immaculate words." They say that last part with such rapture.

Actually, I believe Shakespeare is to literature what Michelangelo was to sculpture, what Reubens was to painting. The question I raise is: "If Shakespeare is as great as we think (and he *was* a master story-teller), then why not modernize his writings, take out the antequated stuff and revamp with present-day words? Is it because then everyone could read Shakespeare and enjoy him, and the scholars would no longer have a monopoly on esoteria? No, the reason Shakespeare hasn't been updated is because it wouldn't sell. The average public wouldn't buy it. I say this with the full knowledge that the book market is a tough business, and anything as well known as Shakespeare's works would have been snapped up and modernized years ago if there were a market for it. There are publishers who don't give a hang *who* they slander if there is a market for it. Thus we are assured there is no great mass market for Shakespeare.

The major reason English departments fail to turn out writers— writers worth reading— is because they suppose that one learns to write by studying great writers. Whereas the truth is, if you're going to learn to write— you must write. Then you must write some more, and when you catch your breath, you had better write a few hundred more stories. That is the way one learns to write. Also one must have something worthwhile to say.

Next to poetry, linguistics is my favorite wrath. Linguistics, to the unfamiliar, is a study of languages— a history of languages. One's first encounter with a scholar of linguistics will leave one weak from the startling revelation that one human, even a professor, can uncover and manufacture so much mouthwash and project it at a classroom full of students.

Linguistics classes begin with a plodding gait, then get gradually but steadily worse as the semester drags on. A linguistics professor can make eternity seem like a welcome relief. First, he takes a unit called a phoneme, which is the smallest single sound. He will take A for example, or E, two letters that never did him any harm, and see how many ways he can pronounce them and twist them around and bend them out of shape. And what does it all amount to? Who cares! Lord, Lord, friend, it don't mean a thing to nobody but the poor ass who's teachin' the class. The only use for linguistics is to teach. It serves *no* useful purpose whatsoever. The scholar will tell you it is the forerunner to future modification of the language. That is a whopper. New words enter the language through science and slang. Word-coiners do not consult a linguist to see if they are allowed to use the word. Society decides what words are going to be used in speech. "Hung" was for years incorrect, "hanged" being the correct word. Today any English teacher not stranded in the antequated past will verify that he no longer has that hang-up.

May I exhibit two shining examples of the value of linguistics? The linguistics scholar's favorite proverb is, "the dictionary is not always right." I suppose that means we must go to the scholar for the absolutely correct plumbing of a word? Does that give you the feeling that we're all out of step but the scholar? Think about it.

The greatest imbecility I ever witnessed was in a linguistics class. The professor asked five students to go to the board and diagram (break into the smallest component sounds) twenty words each; a total of one hundred words. The students did it and the professor critiqued each word. For one serious moment, let me state that the professor could read only *seven* of those words! Only nine of the words were ascertained to be diagrammed incorrectly. But the instructor had to ask what most of the words were. Then he would say, "Oh yes. Yes, that looks right."

When I could stand it no longer, I asked, "Sir, if *you* must ask what the word is, then of what value is linguistics to the class— or to society?"

I'll never forget his condescending look. Then, with the complacency of a man holding four aces, he said:

"Linguistics helps us to better understand the language."

I retire. How could I improve on that kind of sublime ignorance?

And now a word about poetry.

Some years ago, when I was laboring to become an English scholar, I got railroaded into an obscure literature class. They told me I needed the course. I know now the advisers for English majors were padding the class because they could not get enough students to enroll of their own free will.

I struggled along with that miserable course. Every time I came out of that class I would tear up twenty yards of shrubbery. I tell you, I never was so glad as when I found out that all the great Scottish poets are dead! It was *such* a relief to me. Poetry begins with two old renegade Englishmen who should have been retired long ago: Chaucer and Beowulf. After one has suffered through the torments of the damned reading those old tales, one proceeds on to the Scottish poets. A professor of literature can get pretty heated up over Scotch poetry. I don't doubt some of them would read it for breakfast— if they thought somebody was peeking. One must understand Scottish poetry to appreciate it. But more important, one must understand Scotchmen. I acquired a sufficiency of Scotch blood in my lineage, thus I am as qualified as any to discuss the Scots and Scotch poetry. Scotchmen wrote poetry because they were too cheap to write prose. Times were hard in

Scotland in those bygone days and pencils and paper were a luxury rather than a necessity. So the Scots wrote poems, which were much shorter as to line and length than the longer, more expensive prose. The Scots were the first to write on restroom walls (in pubs)— it saved paper.

But there is another factor entering into Scottish poetry. There is a distinct relationship between Scotch poetry and Scotch whiskey. The question is: in what portions should the two be mixed to get the best results? And in what quantity should they be consumed to acquire the best benefits of each? One might assume that equal amounts of each might be a fair proportion, but my own research indicates that the more whiskey consumed, the better the poetry gets. We need more research in this problem. I was going to read some Scotch poetry to my cat once, but when I got warmed up and begin to babble, why, he crawled under the bed and refused to come out until I promised that I wouldn't read any more to him.

I know something about poets because I have photographed several. For instance, I know it takes, on the average, a quart of whiskey a day to run their machinery. But I have discovered something else about poets. They are incomplete human beings— unfinished. They didn't get their final coat of varnish and their brains escaped through an open pore in their skin.

When I expire I am leaving behind a trust fund to assist those who wish to eliminate poets.

*Family relations and child development:* In this branch of study there is a three hour course entitled "Child Development." The course outline reads: "An introductory study of the child from conception through adolescence." Taught by Professor Lovejoy, Dr. Lovejoy, *Miss* Lovejoy— a spinster. Be that as it may, there is not a one of us but must agree that the coverage of the subject seems to be thorough. It would strain the imagination to begin any earlier in a child's development.

Another class that offers food for thought is "Family Relations," taught by Hickey. Doubtless Hickey is assisted in the class instruction by Professor Lotsa Foreplay, a lady who comes with excellent recommendations.

On behalf of the departments of family relations and child development across the nation, may I say it is generally felt they do a great deal more practical good than do the departments of educational psychology.

*Finance:* In too many cases the professors of finance are scholars who know everything in their field— except how to apply it. The ones who know how to apply the successful theories of finance are helping to acquire the capital which pays the taxes that runs the schools. Thus the finance professor is assured of a job for yet another year.

*Foods and nutrition:* There are few schools in the nation recognized for their excellent nutrition departments. This is good, for it keeps the good instructors in close contact with one another. Nutrition, while coming into its own in recent years, has been regarded as a humble study. Doctors, in order to maintain their high level of sophistication and superior knowledge, have regarded themselves as the recognized authorities of nutrition, when in fact it is possible for a medical student to graduate from any of several medical schools without ever having to take a course in nutrition. At most, a medical school will require only three hours of instruction in nutrition, whereas a registered dietitian must spend five years learning her specialty.

*Foreign languages:* Should be reserved for foreigners.

*Geology:* Someone should do a concentrated, in-depth study of "leavemrites." Leavemrites, in the geologist's terminology, are those rocks of unknown origin and description. When a geologist is in the field and runs across such a rock it is customary to "leave-'em-right-there." Otherwise their classification can be most troublesome and more bother than they seem worth.

*Health, physical education and recreation:* This formerly was a dumping ground for retarded athletes. When they eventually graduated— often without ever opening a book— they dashed out to become coaches.

Today, HPER is a touch school. A degree in the discipline involves studies in applied anatomy and rinesiology, motor activities for the educationally handicapped, and laboratory of assessment of human capacity.

Then, of course, there are the other courses: swimming for beginners, beginning horseback riding, gymnastics, badminton, archery, pool hustling, underwater basket weaving, and coeducational wrestling. Yes, all the old difficult courses are still there.

*History:* At the institution where I am presently doing time, the history department has 248 hours— it just goes to show how a good department head can grow cactus on his windowsill.

*Housing and Interior Design:* This is one of the most interesting of studies, yet no man worthy of the name will venture near the subject. It is no secret that the study of interior design has a strong attraction for the *thin-wristed* ones; almost as strong as they have for one another.

While many of the creative masterpieces concocted by these lads and ladies are a marvel to behold, they work with the firm realization that they do not have to endure the results for an extended period of time. Only the patron paying the bill has to live with their creations. Granted, most decorating schemes are artfully done and many are tastefully done. But there is a substantial difference between *seeing* one of these marvels of design and *living* with it.

Walls, draperies, carpets are, perhaps, best selected by an "artistic one," but when it comes to who's going to select the chair I sit in or the art that I must look at, there is likely to be a showdown.

*Journalism:* This is another section of the academic world where I have made my home from time to time.

Journalism, as a trade, is a noble, if somewhat underpaid, profession. That is to say, the good journalists are usually underpaid. *Most* journalists are overpaid at any price. I submit tomorrow morning's paper as evidence. Facts, dreary facts, that is what the aspiring journalistic genius is instructed to bring back. How many morning newspapers are written to enlighten and entertain? How many are written with the idea of sending you off to work with a smile on your face and a spring in your step? Here is today's paper: IS WAR IMMINENT IN THE MIDDLE EAST? TWENTY-THREE DEAD IN TRAIN DERAILMENT. BOY LOST IN MOUNTAINS—FEARED DEAD. UNION LEADER JAILED. MAYOR

AND CITY COUNCIL IN DEADLOCK. Is this wonderful news? Is this information that makes you want to go out and "love thy neighbor?" Well, hardly. Most news is written like this:

SHOOTING STABBING IN TAVERN

At approximately 11:20 last night a gruesome event occurred at a tavern located at 1131 N. 81st. One Jerome B. Johnson was shot numerous times in the chest and abdomen with a large-caliber handgun.

Before he died, Johnson stabbed his assailant, Lemuel Smith, and both men expired in a pool of blood.

Why couldn't the news look like this?

FRIENDLY DISAGREEMENT AT LOCAL INN

There was an addition to the usual entertainment at Friendly Fred's Fuzzy Fox Box on N. 81st last night. The festivities began when Lemuel Smith, a regular patron at Fred's, had over-familiarized himself with the grain and the grape. Smith stood up, steadied himself at the bar and announced that his wife was the "best in town." There was a short reflective silence, and then one Jerome B. Johnson, well known connoisseur of the flesh, jumped up and agreed with Smith. Whereupon Smith, deciding that Johnson was full of hot air, withdrew a .357 gatling gun and ventilated Johnson until he was satisfied. (Smith was slightly more satisfied than Johnson.) Johnson, feeling offended because Smith had ruined his new suit, left.

Presently Johnson returned with a large, well-honed, double-bitted axe and rearranged the component parts of Smith to his entire satisfaction. (Johnson, in this case, was somewhat more satisfied with the results than was Smith.)

We feel it only fair to report that such vigorous exercise overstrained both men and they retired— permanently.

Now, is there any reasonable reason why news could not be presented in such an enlightening and agreeable manner? Would it not be easier to digest one's breakfast if the news were written in an entertaining manner?

If anybody knows how to please a journalism professor, aside from killing him, please let me know. I have turned a story in one semester and received a C on it and turned it in the next semester in a more advanced class and received an A for the effort.

*Management:* This is another example of the scholar knowing everything about the subject except how to do it.

*Medicine:* The dean of a school of medicine, one of the largest and finest in the nation, is a friend of mine. One day, over a hurried sandwich lunch, I asked him if he ever worried about some of the students that graduated from his school?

"Yes," he said, "I do worry about it. As a matter of fact, I wish to God there were some way to keep some of them from ever practicing medicine. But we set up certain standards, and somehow they manage to pass these standards. These questionable ones make their grades and pass all the requirements, so we are forced, by law, to give them their diploma." He sat in a reflective mood for a few moments and then said, "Many's the time I sit up there in my office and hope that none of my family ever has a serious accident in or near the towns where these doctors practice. They would never have a chance to pull through."

Changing the subject, I said:

"I understand Dr. ________ is doing open heart surgery this afternoon. Is it possible for me to observe?" (I was to portray this doctor for a magazine in a few days.) A funny look crossed his face and he said:

"I'm afraid that would be impossible."

"But why?" I asked, somewhat surprised. "You have those wonderful observatories above the operating rooms. Why can't I watch?"

"The observatories have been closed for an indefinite period," he said.

"What? Closed? How come?"

"We had some problems," he replied.

"Really, what kind of problems?" I asked pointedly. "Come on, out with it."

"Well," he began, "as you know, the observatories were built for the observing of operations. However, the observatories were not supervised, except when a medical class was in attendance." He paused for effect, then continued, "as you have no doubt noticed, a great many med students bring their lunch, brown-bagging, I believe they call it. We discovered that the observatories were choice eating places for the brown-baggers. They would bring a date and sit and watch whatever operations happened to be scheduled and consume their sandwiches and coffee. Well, it was just awful. But what brought our attention to these unsupervised periods was the complaint from a young coed that she got pregnant in one of the observatories. She claimed her boyfriend, a med student, promised to show her a 'sex-change' operation and thus lured her up there late one afternoon." My friend looked depressed.

*Microbiology:* Much of our progress in medicine is a result of the science of microbiology. Obviously, medicine has taken giant strides in the last twenty years, and especially the last ten years. We look with pride upon what our scientists have accomplished. We pat ourselves on the back just because we happen to be of the same species as the demigods who made the discoveries. What we fail to realize is that these mighty scientists have the same faults, the same petty insecurities, as the rest of us mortals.

The scientists have been working diligently in recent years for a positive cure for cancer. What we don't realize is that there are dozens, if not hundreds, of scientists working on the same project. Each man works feverishly in his own laboratory, for what— to help mankind? Certainly not! That high virtue escaped him long ago. No, now he works for his own vanity. He desires, more than anything else, recognition. Yes, recognition from his peers drives him on. To hell with humanity. That kind of pussyfooting is for the press— for public relations.

*Music:* For simplicity, if not brevity, let us divide music on the university level into three categories: voice, orchestra, and band.

It is doubtful that there is *one* honest voice teacher in the American educational system. In fact, I am sure of it. For no voice teacher who tells his students the unvarnished truth would hold his job for long. Countless are the times I have been on photographic assignments at universities in the late spring or summer when the windows were open and I could hear students floundering through their voice lessons. Once, only once, did I ever hear a great voice, a really supreme voice, a voice that thrilled, that plucked the spine. Wandering vagrants on campus stood silently in rapture, enthralled at the magnificent sound of that sweet voice. One could not help but feel he was in the presence of greatness! I believe each of us present felt like removing the hat that we were not wearing, or removing our shoes, or something. Just standing there, like a sponge, absorbing the beauty of the sound seemed so, so inadequate. I have often wondered where that lovely nightingale is now. Probably contentedly singing to a toilet bowl, as she scrubs it, while listening with one soft ear for the sound of a sleeping waif in the other room.

Otherwise, the sounds grating from voice classes are barely endurable, at best.

The urge to kill has never been so strong as when I hear some pathetic soul trying to sing the scale with a voice that is flatter and tinnier than a beer can in a busy intersection. One particularly atrocious voice comes to mind. The last time I heard sounds like that was as a boy, when the town's only convalescent home burned.

I would have gladly killed someone to end all our misery. But who was to blame, the young lady with the tennis-shoe voice or the voice coach who refused to tell her it was hopeless? Somehow I felt it was the voice coach who was guilty, so why bother? I would be gone in a day or two, but he had to endure that intolerable noise two or three times a week. Killing would have been a blessed relief. So I let him live, and I don't regret it. He does, but I don't. He happens to be one of the few men I know who is paying for his sins before he goes. Anything hell has to offer should be a welcome change.

Orchestras, on a national average, are excellent. There is much competition for the position of college or university orchestra leader. Only the good ones survive. For the most part they are hard-working, dedicated, industrious men.

But the band, the marching band is where it's at. If you think a college football scrimmage is tough, then you have never watched a really good band work out. If you think a head football coach is tough and mean and overbearing and merciless, then you've never watched a dedicated band leader drive his troops.

The first time I watched a band practice was one afternoon in early fall. I was at a big university in the deep South. When I arrived at the dusty, vacant field where they were to practice, it was a hundred and one in the shade— and they did not march in the shade.

The members, a hundred and twenty-six strong, were uncasing and tuning up their instruments. I'm not sure what the wheezing, whining and wailing of tuning-up does, but it is the most disheartening collection of noises any genius could assemble. I'm satisfied that if the band could be allowed to tune up within hearing distance of the opposing team's dressing room, the demoralization would be total.

Listening to those kids getting their reeds set, and blowing the cobwebs out of their horns, created doubts that they could ever organize into a unit of sound. The members were dressed appropriately for the weather— cut-off jeans and tee-shirts in a rainbow of colors, with an interesting selection of slogans printed on them. There were also the customary assortment of emblazoned patches sewn on in a random fashion. One twirler had a bright red cherry sewn on the fly of her cut-off jeans— a doubtful advertisement at best.

The band director was a curiosity. Let's call him Jussepi Flugeski. He was a Polish-Italian, big, burly, broad-shouldered, but with feminine hands. Comfortable sandals adorned his feet while large, bell-bottomed pants, advertising Coca-Cola, flapped casually as he shuffled along, punting small rocks and clods out of his way. In startling contrast to the sweltering conditions, he wore a baggy grey V-necked sweater with the sleeves pushed up— an Italian's protest to the weather, I presume. Swarthy features masked a handsome, if somewhat aging, face. Pale blue eyes shifted between humor and a fiery temper, while an explosion of curly locks decorated his crown. Little rivulets of sweat trickled through his greying sideburns and down his neck to be soaked up by the sweater. Aimlessly absorbed in thought, his feet practicing the little game of kicking choice rocks aside, he made his way to a tall metal tower. The tower is used by the director for the same reason a coach uses one— to see the pattern of the plays— or maneuvers, in this case.

Having climbed aboard the tower, the director, with a voice like thunder and lightning, called the multitudes together. They came running from all points of the field and collected in a loose group below. Each member looked up at the director in, if not fevered rapture, at least a respectful silence. The director in turn stared down upon his subjects and doubtless thought of himself as their leader, their master, their sole source of inspiration.

A general powwow was held and the problems to be worked on were outlined. I took the opportunity to make some observations. There were, of course, tall kids and small kids, fat kids and lean ones. And a substantial selection in between. There were boy kids and girl types, some black, and some white. There did not seem to be any breakdown between these variations, however. The striking thing which was plain even to me was that the girl whose waist size approximated the business end of a tuba played a piccolo. Whereas the little fella who couldn't weigh a hundred and twenty got to trundle the tuba. Some thought should be given to such situations, for there is a potential danger there. If a strong gust of wind should catch the tuba full force, there is a good possibility that the person playing the instrument could be blown away. Or at least tumbled around like a tumbling weed. This could result in injury to the tuba. Schools furnish these instruments for the band and I believe our tax investment would be in safer hands if we harnessed more piccolo players as tuba tooters. What these instruments need is more base, a heavier anchor, so to speak.

The same must be said for bass drums. Invariably the pipsqueak seems to have the particular talent for playing the bass drum. If this is as true as it always seems to appear, then whoever distributes talent has a strange sense of humor. Doubtless if it were necessary to carry a grand piano onto the field, there would be a recruitment program for a ninety-eight pound weakling to do the job.

The director was winding up his pep talk:

"Alright, I wanna see a lotta spirit out there this afternoon, lotsa hustle, unnerstan'? I don't wanna see nobody loafin', got that? Now when you leave here to hit formation you're gonna doubletime! The first person I see walkin' to formation will be sent to the sidelines to work on fundamentals!" (What are they gonna do— a few pushups, maybe?) "Alright now, let's go!"

There was a mass of scurrying like beavers on pep pills as everybody raced for his position in the formation. The order, "instruments ready," was given and a nod from director to drum major triggered a shrill whistle and practice was underway. Band music is most commonly a brisk beat, often calling for doubletime marching and, occasionally, even triple time.

This works a hardship on drummers, who not only have to march to the frantic time, but have to carry a drum four times their size and hammer the beat at the insane pace. Should the drummer ever ease off on the time of the beat, I'm sure the director would run him through with a clarinet or bean him with a flute.

Never have I seen a group driven so unmercifully as that band was. The temperature climbed to a hundred-and-three. The sweat poured off those kids. Tee-shirts became soaked and clung to interesting female shapes, yet the guys in the band were too tired to notice. Sweat streamed down and into eyes, hair became matted, everybody looked exhuasted. Every fifteen minutes a new drummer was run in, sort of a substitution system, and the relieved one staggered over to the sidelines and slumped down, soaking wet. Meanwhile, with the relief drummer, the band thundered off on a new tack, picking up speed as they went.

All the while, the director was shouting directions through a bullhorn. Now and then he would stop the band and correct some fault or other:

"Whatsa matta, your horn gotta cold? Well, give it two aspirins and it better sound better when we get back on the field! Shirley, I see a face and I see some fingers, but I don't hear any noise. You better start getting some air through that horn if you plan to travel with this band! Alright now, let's run through formation number sixteen, and I wanna see some *life* out there."

I guess they ran defensive plays for a while or something. Finally a ten minute rest was declared and most members collapsed in their tracks. Water was not allowed but gum was passed around, and if oxygen had been available, it would have been a welcome relief. Horns were salivated, a blister on the drum was patched and a list was made of the injured— one drum hernia. It was not specified whether it was the drum itself or the drummer who was afflicted.

One twirler appeared about five months pregnant. Some of the twirlers appeared overly plump, while others were too thin, but they averaged out pretty well.

The exhausting pace continued for an hour and fifty minutes, with only short intervals for catching up with such necessities as breathing. I have never seen any athletic team workout harder and with more diligence. I suspect many a school's band puts on a finer performance on Saturday afternoon than does the team it is supporting. Next time you are watching a band perform its intricate maneuvers with its customary precision, reflect a moment on the home team score. Perhaps it would be an improvement to transfer the band director over to the coaching staff for a season or two.

*Pharmacy:* My knowledge of pharmacy is limited. My knowledge of pharmacists, however, is less limited. The dean of a fine school of pharmacy is a personal friend, and a patron of my photography. (That helps our friendship along considerably.) One day, when I was in the process of bilking him into a fresh portrait, I asked him if he ever worried about the quality of the students they graduated.

"Worry about them? Listen, when I'm up there having to hand out diplomas at graduation, instead of saying 'congratulations' to some of them, I want to say, 'God be with you.' Honestly, I sit up nights wondering how they keep from poisoning someone!"

*Philosophy:* Whenever the word *philosophy* intrudes itself into my consciousness, I always remember the want ad I once saw: "Ph.D. in philosophy wants job washing dishes." Probably a put-up ad, but nevertheless interesting. In my travels it was my questionable pleasure to meet and photograph some learned philosophers. What, one might ask, did I garner from these magnificent minds that I could pass on to those who labor along on my own level? Very little. Nothing truly worth repeating. None of these men were modern day Aristotles. None seemed to be overflowing with vast rivers of wisdom. All seemed to be exceptionally well read and each was capable of spouting volumes of philosophy from his favorite long-dead philosopher, yet one could not help but notice that not one of these men had any defined philosophy of his own. It seemed to me that each was nothing more than a well-read parrot. An eighth-grader, reading into a tape recorder, could store the same knowledge, and do it cheaper. If one does not have the capacity of astute observation, no amount of classroom training can ever make a worthwhile philosopher. Only a "heap-o-livin' " makes a philosopher. No, I would rather listen to the spit-n-whittle club at a crossroads store in the back settlements of most any state than have to listen to the tiresome prattle of a philosopher.

*Photography:* Photography schools consist of a collection of instructors who are incapable of making a respectable living at photography. Most schools of photography are dedicated to the modern idea of abstract photography. *Trash-can photography,* serious, successful photographers call it. It earned its just and deserved name because that is where the results of this particular brand of photography belong.

The faculty of photography schools, not having had to hustle a job or a commission in recent years, have no idea how to prepare a graduate in the art of seeking employment. Of the scores of graduates whom I have met, not *one* had a really first-class portfolio that presented his work in a manner that would properly impress a prospective client. It is not the student's fault, for he comes to the school in blissful ignorance. Unfortunately, he is allowed to graduate with an only slightly modified form of the same collection of ignorance.

*Political science:* Mark Twain, in one of his truly luminous moments, said: "Politics only draws third-class intellects." If that is true, and history certainly has the look of it, then think of the intellectual poverty that staffs a typical political science department! Watch closely when old Professor Smoothbore lectures on the duties of the president. As he drones dully along, doing his best to gas the class into eternity, you can see his eyes glaze over and he gets a seraphic look about him. Practically every political science professor is a flunk-out in the rough game the "big boys" play. Actually, they never had the guts to go out and play the big leagues.

*Psychology:* There are those of us who argue the question, "Does psychology attract those who are slightly crazy, or do they become slightly crazy *after* they get into psychology?" Some claim it's one way, some think it's the other. Whatever, there are some strange people in psychology and related fields.

Psychology has been around for several years now. And in all that time those psychologists have unearthed only one major fact, only one fact worth putting down on paper. What is it? It's the fact that *everybody's different!* Isn't it wonderful that the study of the mind recruits such genius? Isn't it exciting that they discovered this magnificent fact all alone, and without the help of the more dismal sciences? Well, they didn't actually discover it all by themselves. When I was a small boy my grandmother used to tell me people were different, and I believed her. She was basically a truthful person and her theory seemed plausable at the time. I have yet to find any defect in it.

What psychology has managed to achieve is a magnificent grasp of the perfectly obvious. But in order to retain an air of scholastic competence among peers, psychologists use ponderous restatements masked by a smokescreen of jargon. Psychologists have a marvelous capacity for making the simplest truth unfathomably obscure.

It is true that there are some experiments which should not be run on humans without first testing on lesser creatures. However, rats have been running mazes for years and years now. Isn't it time somebody became suspicious of just how much knowledge can be gained from rats running mazes? Many problems given to rats do not even sufficiently test the intelligence of the rat.

There is an established fact in the field of child psychology that a first-grader's interest span is shorter than five minutes. Now, any person not asleep can tell you that the consuming interest of a first-grade boy is recess. And that his mind is never far from the thoughts of the recess bell.

At one time a substantial portion of my business came from photographing distinguished doctors for two national medicine magazines. One day I was to photograph one of the great research psychiatrists of the world. A man, they assured me, who had contributed much to present-day psychiatry.

Our appointment was for two-thirty. I arrived early and set up my equipment. The large institution had been kind enough to lend me the use of a library of rare medical books for the series of portraits I was to do. I never bother a man unless he is thirty minutes late. The gentlemen with whom I am privileged to work are busy and important, otherwise I would not be commissioned to portray them— so I like to tell myself. Be that as it may, my subject was some forty minutes late. I picked up the phone and dialed his office. A secretary answered:

"Hello, this is the photographer who is to do Dr. ________'s portrait. I was wondering if he had forgotten our appointment, or if he is busy and cannot get away at the moment?"

"I'm sorry, Sir, Dr. ________ is on his way to the library," the secretary replied.

"Perhaps he is not familiar with the location of the library?" I said. For the library was across the street from the hospital proper. It was bitter cold outside and most of my patrons used a heated tunnel, which ran beneath the street, to reach the library.

"No," she said, ". . . I have a confession to make. Dr. ________ is somewhat absent-minded. He left here almost an hour ago so that he would be on time for his appointment with you. However, he keeps meeting acquaintances and stopping to chat. When he does, he forgets where he is headed. Then he has to call back to the office and ask me where it was he's going. He's called three times now. He *should* be there any minute now."

While she was making her apologetic explanation, a slightly built little man in a white lab coat ambled into the room, as if lost, and absently began browsing among the collection of books.

I thanked the secretary and asked her if her boss had stark white hair that was not on familiar terms with a comb? She answered to the affirmative and I told her that unless one of the patients was loose, her boss had just arrived. I went over, extended my hand, and said:

"Good afternoon, sir. You must be Dr. ________?"

"Yes, yes I am, er, Dr. ________, and you, you must be the, er, the— ?"

"Yes, Doctor, I am the photographer who is to do your face. Let's step over here and discuss— "

We got along splendidly once he showed up. To this day I believe the man was harmless, if not roused up. Which is more than I can say for the character in this next story:

It was about a month later and I was delivering a large color portrait to a doctor in the neurosurgery department. I was walking down the hall of the psychiatric wing when I met Dr. ________. This man, so I am told, is one of the most famous child psychiatrists of our time.

"Good morning, Dr. ________," I greeted him, as I walked briskly down the hall. He gave me a questioning glance, then recognized me and returned the greeting with friendly interest. The good doctor swung around, put his arm about my shoulders and strolled along with me:

"Say, my friend, that was a mighty fine portrait you did of me the other day."

"Why thank you, Doctor," I replied, "that is very gracious of you to say so."

"Yes," he continued, "my wife saw the proofs and she thinks they are splendid!"

"I am delighted she liked them," I said.

"I was wondering— would it be possible for me to purchase a print for my wife?"

That was like asking Smokey the Bear if he likes the forest:

"Certainly," I answered.

"Fine! Let's step into my office, here, and talk about it."

We went into his office and discussed the purchase price. Soon it became apparent that my idea of a reasonable robbery and his idea of a good deal were some little distance apart— like a couple of light years.

I was not hurting and didn't particularly care whether he ordered or not. He could easily afford the price, if he wanted the picture. He warmed to the one-sided argument and tried to explain, as if talking to a child, how the price was perfectly ridiculous. Presently, seeing that his attack was having no appreciable effect on the leather-headed victim, he tried another approach. He threw himself on the floor and screamed and hollered and cried and kicked the furniture and threw a temper-tantrum that would have been instructive to the most shameless five-year-old. I looked around. "What the hell," I thought, "is this performance solely for my entertainment? Or is there someone else here to help enjoy this spectacle? What if somebody should come in?" I thought. Then I figured, "It's his show. If someone comes in, *I'm* not the one screaming and kicking around in little circles and chewing on a lamp cord. What's it to me if somebody walks in?"

Presently he ran out of steam, as tantrums and other calamities are likely to do if not encouraged. He sat up, then pulled himself into an upright position, straightened his hair, his tie, and dusted himself off. Then he extended his hand and thanked me most cordially for my time and expressed his sorrow that we couldn't do business together. I was ushered to the door and once more found myself standing in the hall.

I do wish somebody would volunteer and explain to me why he did that. It has been a considerable burden to me.

So much for psychology and its related studies. Perhaps we are better off if the shrinks *do* stay in the laboratories and play with the other animals.

*Religion:* There seems little value in poking fun at religion, and thus courting the likelihood of getting singed by lightning. The Diety has a way of getting back at one when the repayment is least expected. He and I are harboring strained relations toward one another right now, so perhaps it is best if I skip lightly over religion and religious schools.

Seminaries. They do seem to have a biased opinion don't they? Also, they only seem to project the good side. Think how their enrollment would jump if they ever decided to present the sinful side too, as a contrast. After all, most of us were taught how to be good. But how many of us ever had a single lesson on how to be bad? Most of us have had to learn the hard way, self-taught. And what a poor teacher most of us were to ourselves. Most of us can't even lie without getting caught. But I had better ease up. I just heard it thunder. Probably no relation to my efforts, but it is better to be safe, and go find a low, inconspicuous area. After all, most kids who enroll in theology classes or attend religious schools weren't forced to do so.

*Reserve Officers Training Corps (ROTC):* Land-grant schools, because of their affiliation with federal funding and grants, must offer courses in what the school catalogs discreetly refer to as "Defense." Isn't that sweet.

I would complain loud and long about such classes which teach the principles and techniques of war, except that every society from time immemorial has a certain small percentage of men who are fascinated by the immense challenges of war. It is a small but substantial flaw in the construction of the human race. It *seems* strongest in the Christian nations. But perhaps this is an inaccurate observation. It is likely that it is only a trait of the most highly civilized.

I have photographed and talked with several generals of the armed forces. It was their opinion, to a man, that the national defense budget was dangerously low, and that it was impossible to defend a country of this size on such a miserly budget. It was also their considered opinion that each man was bred for the sole purpose of serving as a pawn in someone's army. It would take a separate volume, printed on asbestos, to do full justice to that kind of reasoning.

*Sociology:* Today's young generation, intent on reforming the world, peacefully preferably, has swarmed into the discipline of sociology to cure the world's problems. What they succeeded in doing was overpopulating the field. After graduating and discovering that almost every upstanding young boy and girl had the same idea, and that there are sixty applications for every job offer for a sociologist, the graduate takes a job as a secretary, or sacks hamburgers— and becomes part of the problem he set out to mend.

# 9

# Administration

What I have been trying to show by illuminating some of the many disciplines is that much of what is presented as knowledge is not needed at most colleges or universities. Most schools could improve their curriculum simply by selectively dropping half of the courses they offer. How would this help? First, it would eliminate half the teachers, maybe more. We would assume, even pray, that it would eliminate the less desirable half. Less space would be required, meaning better facilities at a lower cost.

"So where, Dummy," the educators are saying, "do you propose to make the dropped classes available to those students who want to take them?"

Many classes could be incorporated into others without doing damage to the subjects. Indeed, the way most classes are taught, nobody would notice the difference. As for those *dropped* classes, in every state there are a few large universities where these classes could be lodged. Also it is conceivable that half a dozen large universities across the nation could take care of the demands of some advanced subjects such as astronomy, meteorology, linguistics, advanced nuclear engineering, etc. There is no reason why a student should begin and finish his college career at *one* school. The state in which I am presently going to school has twenty-three state colleges. Why couldn't the better instructors in, say, English, history, home economics, etc., be corraled at one school— along with the most competent instructors in those fields? Then at another school they could specialize in pharmacy and medicine. At still another, agriculture, and at still another, engineering. This could be carried out to a reasonable conclusion, with the student having the benefit of the finest instructors his state could afford.

But there are some holes in this all-encompassing net. The largest hole is pride. Each college, each school of any size, has its pride. Every school wants to be important. Most schools want to increase their enrollment. Then the president of the school can say with pride, "look what *we* did!" Meaning of course, "look what *I* did!" The alumni want to say, "look how our school has grown!" And every dean and every department head wants his department to be more prestigious. How do you appear more prestigious? Being larger is one accepted way. The larger the department, the more prestige it has. The larger the departments, the larger the school. The larger the school the more important it becomes. You see how it is— a vicious circle. The alumni pressure the president for a bigger, better school. The president turns to his vice presidents and deans, who in turn lean on the heads of the respective departments. The *word* is enlarge, expand, get more students, recruit, Recruit, RECRUIT! Thus it is that we have more classes than we need, taught by too many teachers who lack ability as good classroom instructors. What do we do?

All this recruiting, all this encouragement to go to college, has resulted in over-education, over-specialization. Too many students in the fields or art, history, education, sociology, psychology, and engineering are no longer able to find jobs when they graduate.

It seems to me it is the responsibility of the nation's educational system to inform students that there are no jobs available in certain disciplines. This over-education in certain fields is not a benefit to the nation and certainly no benefit to the graduating student. If the student is self-confident—or stupid— enough still to desire to major in that field, he should be allowed to do so. While students should be abundantly informed of the conditions, we have no right to interfere with their freedom of choice.

# 10

# It Pays to be Black

Obviously it does not pay *everybody* to be black, for certainly those living in the slums do not rejoice that they are black. But if you are a young black student with average intelligence and some ambition, and you are in college, baby, it does pay to be black. And pays well— very well. The black student in graduate school is a prize possession for *any* college or university. The more black students in graduate school, the better. For then the university can stand up, wave its grey flag to the government and say, "hey, look! We have our quota of blacks! We're doing our part— how about more federal grant money?" And the government reaches deeper into your pocket and mine and forks over yet more government aid, as a way of patting the university on the head and saying, "Good work, son."

As the present saying goes, "How *much* does it pay— to be black?" Two examples will suffice: at a large college in the Southwest, I was acquainted with a black graduate student who is a *teaching aid* in the English Department. There are thirty-seven teaching aids in the department. The highest salary paid to *any* of these graduate assistants is a poverty-stricken $240. One student aid draws the enviable salary of $500 a month: my black acquaintance.

There was a vacancy in the Education Department of a sizable Midwestern university not long ago. The head of the department was informed by the president that he could offer $11,500 to fill the position— or $15,000 if the professor were black. Weeks passed, and dragged into months. No black man could be found. Finally there was word that a professor from an all black college in the deep South was interested. His qualifications were adequate, and in their haste to acquire this rare specimen they offered him the job and the whole $15,000— by telegram. He accepted— by telegram. The president and the head of the department were still patting themselves on the back for their brilliance in this most excellent coup when the professor arrived— and was *WHITE!* The professor was innocent, but that was probably one of the lowest, dirtiest tricks ever played on an administration. The head of the department told me he had to fill out six forms, in triplicate, telling why he did not hire a member of a minority race for the position. Who wanted to know? Our government, of course.

The black man who has survived in whitey's world knows something that his brothers in the ghetto haven't yet discovered. One must conform to live in whitey's world. Whitey himself is the greatest conformer of all. He has made a very rigid and exceedingly strict set of laws by which he stringently abides. True, the laws favor whitey. But that is understandable— whitey is the majority.

Most of the requests by the black students to college and university administrators are for space, such as an Afro-American Center in the Student Center or Student Union building. Other requests are for parties, dances, or special Afro-studies courses. *Most* such requests are granted by a college or university. Perhaps these special privileges are regarded by the black student as a social gain. It *might* interest them to know it pleases whitey a great deal to know that he can find the Afro-students clustered in a convenient bunch.

# 11

# If All Else Fails, Read the Instructions

Some people suffer from the habitual practice of never reading instructions— *any* instructions. It is not a profitable custom and can get one into a great deal of trouble. Personally, I have never been afflicted with that particular handicap. I've read instructions on everything from how to smoke a pipe to how to remove my own appendix.

But what do you do if there are no instructions available? Suppose, for instance, you got hit by a stray arrow from a lone Indian who hadn't heard about the ceasefire of 1887? Once the tickling stopped and the interest wore off, why, you would naturally want to remove the shaft. An arrow jutting out of one's person, while interesting enough and certainly a conversation piece, would doubtless become a nuisance after a time. Once the novelty wore off, it seems one might tend to acquire certain peculiar, inhibiting traits. Anybody can see it would cause the beginnings of a complex the first time somebody walked up and hung his hat on your spike. Perhaps it has not occurred to you lately just how tough it is to get proper instructions on the removal of a flinthead arrow. And without adequate instructions the job could soon cease to be entertaining. The hoary old maxim, "if in doubt use a bigger hammer," would be in poor taste to a dying man.

Now let me give you a more serious view of the problems that arise from lack of instructions. Two or three years ago, while meandering through the local supermarket, I discovered a new beverage, new to me anyway, eggnog. It was the holiday season and being in a festive mood I purchased a quart of the stuff. It was delicious! A few days later I overheard somebody say that eggnog was improved a great deal by the addition of a little spirits. That certainly sounded feasible. I had long believed that whiskey would improve anything from toothpaste to shoe polish. I loosened my belt another notch and purchased two more quarts of eggnog. Unfortunately, nobody informed me that eggnog, in sufficient quantities, has the same general effect on the human system that dynamite has on a logjam. That night I prepared to concoct myself a small nightcap of eggnog with a little *relaxer* in it for medicinal purposes. Had I known then what I am sadly aware of now I would have proceeded with more caution.

However, with blissful ignorance, I took down a small glass and was about to pour in the eggnog— but how *much?* Simple enough, read the instructions. Hum-m-m-m, I read the whole carton and there was not one word about how much liquor one should add. At least it certainly wasn't printed on the *outside* of the container. Well, no problem, it shouldn't be too difficult to arrive at the proper blend. I poured in equal amounts of eggnog and— and tequila. I happened to be out of legitimate liquor at the time. Took a drink. It was a prime and vivid example of greased lightning. It slipped down easy enough, but it devastated everything in its path, tongue, throat, stomach, liver, spleen, everything. The damage being done, I reasoned that I might as well continue the experiment. I was not aware, at the time, that it had affected my mind.

I filled the glass with eggnog and tried again. Still no improvement. The fire that raged inside for the next few minutes wiped out everything that had survived the first round. I am blessed with a strange sense of determination and was resolved to finding the proper proportions of this perplexing drink. I got a larger glass and added more eggnog. Sipped it again. It was beginning to modify some. Filled the glass to the brim. Took another pull. It was getting better. Found myself a large iced tea glass, poured in the mixture from the previous glass and dumped in the remains of the quart of eggnog. Tried it again.

Now I had too much eggnog! This was indeed the infernalest mixture I ever tried to get the hang of.

Found a large mixing bowl, dumped in the quart of mongrel brew, grabbed up the tequila and sloshed in about a glass-full.

I kept experimenting with that exasperating mixture until I had used up both quarts of eggnog, the fifth of tequila, a half-gallon of milk, and two-thirds of a bottle of tabasco sauce. I forgot now just why I thought the tabasco sauce would improve matters, but it seemed like a good idea at the time. I had too much invested in the mixture now to dump it out, so being of frugal Scotch blood I drank it, *ALL* of it. At one sitting.

Now, you might labor under the illusion that I was too crocked to move, but you would be mistaken. Unusually mistaken, superbly mistaken, entirely mistaken. Under normal conditions you would have been correct, but eggnog and tequila do not play by the rules. Not by any rules I have ever encountered. Not by civilized rules. Indeed not! No, sir, of necessity I was up from there in a considerable hurry and searching earnestly for a bathroom. I could not remember whether I owned a bathroom or not but someone looks after fools, they say, and in the final frantic seconds I found one. I was not choosy whether it was mine or exactly who it belonged to.

I amused myself with the "Tijuana Two-Step" for the next three or four days. Going to classes was unthinkable. Getting out of the house was out of the question. When "Montezuma's Revenge" finally retreated and left me alone I swore off eggnog. Nor do I plan any further experiences without first acquiring either a recipe or some instructions.

# 12
# Student Dorms

At a large Western university there is a dormitory complex. There is a courtyard in the center and four large five-story dorms face into the courtyard. It is a boy's dormitory complex and, as we know, boys do not keep any neater living quarters than girls. The area got progressively filthier until things got pretty near intolerable for the two or three respectable residents who lived in the complex. A complaint was lodged and members of the university housing administration were sent over to inspect the situation. The findings were unsatisfactory and an order was issued to clean up the place "or else."

A Saturday was set aside for this project and an inspector was assigned to see that the work was accomplished. On the prescribed day everyone fell upon the room-cleaning project with enthusiasm. Rooms were cleaned, trash was removed, beds were made, floors were swept and waxed, dust was dusted and rooms began to gleam cheerfully again.

However, the tons of newspapers, *Playboy* magazines, trash, empty pizza delivery boxes, beer cans, bottles, etc., were swept into the neutral zone, the hallways. And nobody was willing to take the responsibility of sweeping it out. Naturally this condition was not tolerated by the housing administration. So another order was issued to "clean out those hallways." Again the bulk of the labor force was rallied and work began. As top-floor dwellers swept their accumulated trash down to the next lower floor, and the underlings swept it down the stairwells to the next floor, the piles grew to discouraging proportions.

When the combined mess landed on the first floor it was a mountain of almost unmovable dimension. Some resident, disgusted with the futility of it all, unlimbered the *emergency-only* fire hose and proceeded to wash the trash out into the courtyard. The high-pressure hose was much more efficient and entertaining than straining against a broom handle. Seeing such productivity in one dorm, the residents of other complexes copied the idea, and indeed, improved upon it.

One dorm group, being a somewhat civilized, nonathletic tribe, had carried its collected garbage, trash, refuse, etc., out into the courtyard and piled it neatly outside its front entrance. Naturally this orderly conduct was resented in the other complexes. The delights and temptations of evil being what they are, more hoses were uncoiled from upper floors and with the aid of the reinforced power the tidy pile of trash was washed back into the entrance of the virtuous ones.

Retaliation was immediate and vehement. Hoses were unreeled and an unsuspecting swisher of the opposing force was caught unaware by the first powerful blast of water, and knocked end over end by the forceful stream! After that every hose was pressed into action. Sporadic fist fights and some gang fights erupted. These were temporary disturbances, for soon streams of cold water pounded the combatants and discouraged further activity. It is hard to carry on heated physical violence against an icy stream of water.

Police were called and immediately rushed into the courtyard, where they were promptly zapped. Dripping wet and cold to the morrow in their bones, they beat a hasty retreat. One venturesome officer sallied forth, with a bullhorn, to make some forceful suggestions to the residents. He caught a stream of water full-face. They had to use a pry bar to remove the bullhorn from his face. Obviously the students had the heavy artillery. A squishy, sodden police captain called the fire department and through chattering teeth requested its assistance. Once on the scene, the firemen quenched the battle in short order— they cut off the water. With no ammunition, the war was over.

# 13
# Getting High

Drugs. Dope. Hashish. Speed. Pot. Even amphetamines. To a person over thirty, these all sound pretty frightening. A mild high brought on by the delights of wafting pot causes no particular harm, I am assured. Perhaps that is so, but not having tampered with the evidence I am not qualified to dispense a verdict. I have, however, had the opportunity to be personally escorted through the famous Menninger Clinic, in Topeka, where approximately one third of the patients most seriously in trouble are young people who tried to rip their minds to shreds with hard drugs. Those must have been beautiful trips, for those kids haven't come down yet!

*Why,* I kept asking myself, do kids do this to themselves? The answer apparently is boredom: that is the major reason cited by the kids themselves. Okay, fine, boredom, but isn't there *some* way to overcome this boredom without piercing oneself with a needle? There *must* be something. There is alcohol, of course, but the kids have experimented with that and found it inadequate. Besides alcohol is a *downer.* The kids experiment freely with sex, yet I get the feeling they do not have the experience or knowledge to gain the maximum benefit from it; most people never do. Skinny-dipping parties in the summer are fine and naughty but they do not create the high that kids are seeking. What, then, outside of the fantasies of a chemical-induced high, could create the same effect? What experience could one fabricate that would release the mind and let the imagination float free and create its own atmosphere at an unhindered level?

After a sufficiency of unencumbered reflection I hit upon a unique experience that will expand the mind to an amazing degree; indeed, those who have tried both hard drugs and the X-system of Super-Sensual Perception say it takes less pure unadulterated nerve to shoot speed the second time than to follow the system twice.

If you follow my instructions you will find yourself acquiring a gradually rising high that will finally climax on a sustained level that will last for hours. If you have a strong heart, there is no physical danger except, perhaps, what you might do to yourself. Psychologically the only danger is, again, only what you can inflict upon yourself.

I have one of these experiences perfected. Perhaps perfected isn't entirely the correct word, but once involved, you won't notice the difference. Before we go on, however, let us look at the reason hard drugs create a high.

Hard drugs, like heroin, break down a certain chemical in the body which regulates the brain. This chemical regulator acts somewhat as the governor on an automobile. It keeps the brain from racing and destroying itself. By reaching a certain degree of excitement one bypasses this chemical and creates the same type of mind-expanding situation.

Now for the X-system of Super-Sensual Perception: spending an entire night in a graveyard— absolutely alone. If you laugh, you are among the uninitiated, for I assure you the time you spend in a cemetery, on a dark moonless night, will be the most eventful you've ever endured. I speak from the knowledge of vast experience, for surely I am a scholar of *temporary* graveyard residence. Many are the *eternal* nights I have sat with my back to a cold clammy lump of granite and watched the darting shadows play hide-and-seek among the misty forest of tombstones, and listened to the whispers of the wind as it played a strange, haunting tune among the wispy cedars and lonely pines. These are the easy nights, the nights when the local citizens are resting, for the most part, and waiting for more favorable conditions.

I have never spent a truly dull and uneventful night in a graveyard. Even on the most serene of nights something will happen to impress upon you the carelessness of dozing off in such surroundings. There are two classifications of such places: cemeteries and graveyards. Cemeteries, as I see them, are the neat, clean, well manicured, homey little hillsides, generally open in appearance, and divided with loving care and much aforethought into little lots and regimented plots. But the graveyard is a place of grown-up weed, rank undergrowth, leaning, broken, venerable old stones, stained and mossy with age, winding paths, bent, twisted and gnarled trees, uneven ground, vines running everywhere and an atmosphere of macabre disorder.

It is this particular kind of graveyard, usually long abandoned, that will furnish you with the most entertainment and mind-expanding experiences. Indeed, I have come back from some of those places after a particularly dark and stormy night when I couldn't begin to carry my expanded mind home in a bushel basket, and you couldn't have loaded my imagination on two flatcars. I remember one particular evening as if it happened only night before last, yet it has been over six years now. . . .

The graveyard was located on the terrace of a mountain in southern Kentucky, overlooking a deep, narrow, dismal and lonely little valley. I thought the place had potential when I passed earlier in the day. Late that evening I returned with a thermos of gin and soda and a lunch pail of sandwiches and goodies for a midnight snack. For even though I might be so scared I can hardly find my mouth with both hands, I still get hungry on the *graveyard shift* as I prefer to call it. Well it was along about eleven or eleven-thirty and I was sitting there on this little, low, comfortable headstone having an early snack when it began to cloud up pretty sudden-like, and it wasn't long 'til the wind picked up and commenced blowing through the cedars and caused the old dead oak to creak and groan, all spooky and mournful. A drop of rain lit on my cheek, and a dead leaf went clattering by, making more racket than a dozen Hondas on an empty city street. My heart began to pound for I recognized the signs: things were tuning up for a rare evening of thrills and spectaculars. I wasn't disappointed. Before long the wind died down so's you could hear the steady rumble of the heavier artillery being moved into place. Heat-lightning bounced around among the heavy clouds and added luminescence to an otherwise dark and opaque atmosphere. A tumbleweed dashed by, with no gust to propel it. Then suddenly the performance began. The blinding flash of a billion kilowatt bolt of lightning came smoking down from the void and smacked that twisted, gnarled old oak a rattling crash that separated it into component parts and deposited it around the whole area. A mighty clap of thunder shook the mountain and at that instant eight pearly skeletons squirted from their earthly receptacles, each glowing gastly green from the supercharge of electricity to the phosphorus in their venerable bones, and began dancing wildly about. I didn't mind that so much but one of the villains stole my half-eaten sandwich.

If I told you what happened for the next three hours it would spoil the experience for you. I am not one to destroy another man's fun.

There are certain rules to follow if one is to acquire maximum benefit from such an experience:

1. Always go alone. A jittery friend can magnify the horrors and literally scare hell out of you. Besides two imaginations are four times worse than just one. No, go alone. You *might* be able to stay, that way.

2. Do *not* carry a light of any kind. It is best to go before dark and simply let the night close in on you. With a light you will see more than you want to see, and the first time the light strikes a white monument and bounces back it'll scare your navel around to your back side. No, a light is too spooky; leave it at home.

3. Don't drink. It won't help. It hinders. And, besides, you can't run as fast when you're drunk. It is difficult enough trying to get the rhythm of striding over graves in the dead of night without the hindrance of a load of alcohol aboard.

4. Never, never, never take a girl along! I made that mistake one night. Sex was out of the question. She was stiffer than any of the local stiffs. But she did more small things to frighten the living daylights out of me: once when some particularly eerie sound oozed out of the darkness, she grabbed my arm from the opposite side from where I thought she should be. It took us both twenty minutes to find the clothes I jumped out of, and to this day that arm still feels funny on dark nights when I am walking down an unlit alley. No, do not take a girl along. Girls are too spooky.

# 14

# The First Week of School

To the former student who has not haunted a campus for perhaps a decade or so, there have been bits of change wafting along on the breeze of time.

Clothes, of course, are one item that has undergone some *slight* modification. In bygone years it was customary for kids to dress neatly and appropriately for the first day of class. Boys wore "suits" or sports clothes and a tie, while the girls wore suits or neat skirts and blouses. There was even a time when decorum dictated that a girl wear a hat on the first day of school. Today the professor breathes easier to discover that the kids bothered to wear any clothes at all. Many professors live in the mortal fear that someday someone is going to come to his class in a baggie.

Where, before, it was "airs" to meet old friends and appear as your most attractive self (depending upon what you had to work with) today it is "heavy" to look just the opposite. I am convinced, beyond doubt, that companies exist today that survive because they manufacture clothes and then drag them behind tractors until they are sufficiently shabby and threadbare to attract the attention of those young buyers. The first week of school every student is a masterpiece of studied sleaziness. The more strange, the more different, the more picturesque they contrive to be, the more satisfied with themselves they look. If we could arrange to deposit foreign dignitaries on an American campus the second week in September, those dignitaries would return home and begin a foreign aid program to the United States. Many students look like refugees from a care-package center. Religious apparel is *in* at this time. Boys, particularly, prefer religious jeans— very holy. While girls go more for the biblical type blouse— lo-and-behold! Kids today are a curiosity in every way, even to one another. They will stop and exclaim over, and admire, some companion's most recent acquisition, like an old leather-fringed, worm-eaten shot-bag of the Civil War days, which serves as a wallet; or a pair of run-over cavalry boots are a great prize. One-upmanship is the name of the game. If a kid can get the drop on friends by acquiring something particularly novel then he is heavy for some weeks— or until another friend finds something yet more outlandish. An Aussie Digger hat is troop, particularly if one can find it in chartreuse felt! For the girls, shorts with fishnet hose were the thing before cold weather discouraged such brevity. This ensemble was often topped off with the upper portion of a bikini bathing suit— somewhat distracting in class.

A present trend is toward what I refer to as the literary tee shirt. It is camp to find a tee shirt with a really far-out slogan printed on it. There are even shops that will print your very own slogan on your shirt. The more mundane prose will read, "Have a Nice Day," or "Black is Beautiful." But deterioration has arrived and one sees a slogan like "Hump a Hippie." One of the classics is a shirt with the slogan "Fly United" written under a picture of two geese flying while having relations. My favorite is one that a tall, slender, well-built young blonde had on. This lady came to my apartment one cold December afternoon to interview me for some notorious deed I had committed earlier. When she entered, I offered to take her coat. We removed her coat and she had on a pair of jeans and a tee shirt— no bra. On the front of the shirt, in the appropriate locations, were two large M & M's. Under this mildly startling spectacle was lettered THEY WON'T MELT IN YOUR HANDS BUT THEY WILL IN YOUR MOUTH. It was a lie.

Perhaps the strangest single piece of apparel I ever saw was on a New England campus one late spring day. I was there on business, found some free time and proceeded out to the square to watch the kids saunter by. It was relaxing, enlightening and educational in a nonvaluable sort of way. Presently there came a particularly scruffy-looking young character, shoeless, shirtless, shiftless, with bib-overalls, long, unkept, matted hair, ditto for beard, and around his neck, secured by an oily leather thong, a can of sardines. I could either justify, or was indifferent to, all other articles of apparel that had come before— but a can of sardines? I stopped the young vagrant and asked him for a light; asked several casual questions and finally, pointing to the obvious can dangling on his skinny chest, said:

"What's it for?" He looked surprised that one of my ancient vintage could not comprehend such straight and obvious facts.

"Why, Dude," he said, "I'm Pisces!" (The sign of the fish.)

"Of course," I apologized, "how perfectly obvious. How stupid of me."

The students' antipollution movement has induced a congestion of bicycles unfathomable to the noncampus resident. The campus pedestrian is in thirty or forty times more danger from free-wheeling bicycles than he ever was from pollution or auto traffic. These indiscriminate maniacs whiz down busy sidewalks on their ten-speed machines, creating carnage in their wake. Many a campus has found it necessary to mark bicycle lanes on certain sidewalks and roadways in order to create a truce between angry pedestrians and speed-freak cyclists. Especially dangerous is the first week of school at a major university. Thousands of new students converge on campus with bicycles. At first, neither the cyclists nor the pedestrians are familiar with the campus routine. When a cyclist is pedaling, the machine whisks along as silent as a ghost. When the cyclist stops pedaling, the gears start free-wheeling and make a low whining noise. The most vicious sound one can hear while walking peacefully across campus is that low whining noise. Immediately one realizes the cyclist is undecided as to which side he wishes to pass. Your first urge is to step to one side and give the rider room. Then you panic, for the sound is practically in your back pocket and you don't know which way to jump. There is no love between cyclists and pedestrians.

The all-consuming idea of college is to get an education. At least that is what each student tells his parents. How many parents are likely to get excited over the fact that, once on campus, the objective is to tread the thin line between having as much fun as possible, and flunking out?

The two hardest classes for students to attend are those dreadfully early lectures and those four-thirty Friday afternoon labs. By four-thirty Friday all of one's friends are elbowing their way into the assorted local bars where they will proceed to refresh themselves into a formless blob. However, of just recent semesters the trend has swung to Thursday nights. The students play a game among themselves. To my knowledge it has no name, but operates something like this: one goes out and tries to absorb more alcohol per equal capacity than a sponge. It is not important whether a student gets back to his or her quarters or not. But they had better get to class on Friday morning, for it is a mark of large distinction to be able to drag to class. If you make it to class, you receive one point. If you passed out the night before and still make it to class, add two points. If, in addition, you have an hour exam, add five points.

If you don't make it to class you are considered to have crashed and you lose one point. If you do not make it to class 'til the next Tuesday you lose three points and you are listed as trashed-out. Trashed-out is the proper way to gain an enviable standing among the other students. Unfortunately, trashed-out students are usually short-termers. Few of them are perennials on any campus.

In almost any state there is one college known as "flunk-out U.," or "Flunk-Out City." It is sometimes possible for a student to *stay* trashed-out and still acquire a degree from one of these institutions.

In the list of necessary equipment for a student, a car comes considerably before a typewriter. So does a ten-speed bicycle and a four-speaker stereo. At one Texas school there were listed, among the student automobiles, seven new Cadillacs. On the registration cards *Cadillac* was misspelled five times out of the seven.

There was a study done several years ago which proved conclusively that at any given moment 20 percent of the students in any given class were thinking about sex. Carved on half the desks at this school are the words, "I love Marc Allen." It comes as no surprise that Marc Allen is the one perpetuating his own image.

In order really to be a part of the scene at any university today, in order to qualify as a part of the truly "ultra" *in* crowd, you must own a pet. Exotic animals are the most *in*. You can out-do all your friends by riding a Siberian tiger to class. Lacking an exotic pet, the next best thing is a dog. But not just any dog. You can't buy a vote with an ordinary cur. You must either buy or steal a dog that, for size, will shame a small horse. If the dog can't eat ninety dollars worth of groceries every month he doesn't qualify.

Each day the owner of such a beast brings his prize to campus and leaves him in some central location, such as the mall, the green, or a lawn or garden area. The dog stays faithfully in the vicinity until the master comes to take him home. On any given day our campus has from thirteen to twenty-two of these mammoths. St. Bernards are most prevalent, followed by a haired-over version of a sheep dog the size of a four-seated golf cart. Sprinkle in a scattering sample of German Shepherds and you have the picture.

One would naturally assume that there would be need of a referee or two and some scorekeepers to keep up with the frequent dog fights, but not so. The keepers of these brutes are what are called the flower children— hippies, if you prefer— and by some process the dogs have acquired an understanding— a common bond of peaceful coexistence.

These hounds do not merely lie around like docile clumps of landscape, minding their own business. No indeed. For fully half the time they run and romp and rip and tear around with the ferocity of a stampede that would warm the heart of John Wayne. Yet they keep peace in the family. These monsters, weighing from 85 to as much as 240 pounds, play all sorts of games. One of their favorite games is tag, or chase. By some arranged agreement one dog will be the victim while the rest of the pack will tear up acres of lawn chasing after. Each time it happens I expect to see a bloody massacre when the chased dog is caught, but there is never anything but harmony. Students respectfully make way when they see a chase coming their way. Common sense decrees that one stays out of the path, for two or three tons of fun-loving "potlickers" traveling in excess of twenty miles an hour could give one a satisfactory tromping.

Once the chased dog is caught, it is nipped and tumbled and bumped around in a rough but friendly manner. The only time an angry sound is heard is when some member of the pack begins to play too rough. When this happens the pack turns on the offender and he or she becomes the chased.

Seeing those huge canines lumbering along in hot pursuit of one of their companions is a frightening scene, especially considering the stories we hear of domestic dogs forming hunting packs and destroying deer or livestock. Perhaps some of the research expended on rats, gerbils, rabbits and other small fauna could be better used to try and determine why those dogs can live in peaceful playful harmony while their superiors in the animal kingdom are busy creating new and imaginative ways to destroy one another.

I met a transfer student the other day who had just arrived from the University of Minnesota; he said he was from Houston originally. He had taken his tennis rackets with him to Minnesota but instead of playing tennis, he had been forced to use the rackets for snowshoes. He had aspired to be a sculptor but he looked depressed. He told me they only carved ice statues up at the U. of M. and said he had some beautiful sculptures during the fall and spring semester, but they had all melted down to half size during the summer term.

I once put in a few days on the University of Minnesota campus. It was a nice, balmy fifteen or twenty-five below zero at the time. Of all the things that impressed me while there, the thing that was most curious was the winter wardrobe of the coeds. One of their favorite outfits was a large muskrat parka with wolf-skin trimming, heavy gloves of course, and high, lined boots. But for the lower section of the anatomy they wore a popular piece of apparel called *wooly boogers*. Wooly boogers, for the edification of the non-eskimo readers, is a form of hose or tights. These tights are not as comely as the name might imply, for they are heavy wool material. The wool is so pronounced that a girl's legs look like they need shearing. Usually the color is a shaggy brown or a dingy grey. After a few wearings the wool rolls up in little "pills" and looks scruffy as a dead cat. It makes one want to whip out a razor the first few times he sees a pair.

Several years ago, when I was doing my first stretch in school, I got tired of the eternal loudmouth who always showed up at parties, usually uninvited, and claimed he could drink *anything* straight. That was in the days when *liquor* was the major vice at parties— today it's drugs, though liquor is making a comeback.

Well, as I say, I got tired of these party crashers and decided to do something that would entertain me and at the same time get rid of undesirable guests.

I contacted a friend in chemistry and provided him with the necessary ingredients. He brewed up three quarts of liquor distilled from jalipeña peppers. I never tasted it. One whiff would burn the lining out of your nose.

I challenged a couple of wise characters one night. They dropped in on one of my parties uninvited and got to swelling around about how they could drink *anything* that wouldn't eat up the bottle; about how the two of them had killed a quart of white lightnin' apiece one night, and about how—

"'Scuse me," I interrupted quietly, "but I have some spirits you boys can't drink."

"Thas' a lie!" said one, bullying up to me, "I can drink any (ic) any thing that won't rot the bottle!"

"You can't drink this stuff," I said.

"The (ic), the 'ell I can't!" he said. "Trot 'er out here an' I'll chug 'er to the last drop!"

I got the bottle, unscrewed the top and handed it to him.

He took a whiff and looked a good deal impressed— for a drunk.

"Whe-e-e-e-e-w!" he breathed. "Thas' purty strong stuff. Whas' (ic) whas' in it?"

"Straight grain," I lied.

The party crasher screwed up his courage, for a small crowd had gathered, and took a swig.

I met a friend of the party crasher's a few weeks later and happened to ask about him.

"Funny thing," he replied, "Ole Fred quit drinkin' after that night. He said that nip should last him the rest of his life. Last time I saw him, he was moving to Alaska; said he was trying to find a place cool enough for him; said every time he took a drink of water it turned to steam. Said he could stand outside at 115 below zero— nude— and not get frostbite. Said he used to stand it colder, but the effects wuz wearin off."

I can tell I'm not one of the college generation— all modern music sounds alike. Today I heard a record that was, for me, at least, unique. In the background I could hear a garbled, disjointed sound which sounded vaguely familiar, yet somehow I couldn't seem to place it. I believe I have finally isolated the sound now, and can report with authority: the sound is that of someone beating a rooster with a folded newspaper.

Many college libraries have a dress code. The students have to come up to a certain standard of dress before they are allowed in. At one time, at my present school, the dress code read: "Boys must wear dress-shirt and slacks. Girls must wear blouse and skirt; skirt to be not shorter than four inches above the knee." Today the dress code reads: "No swimwear. All students must wear shoes. . . ."

Last semester I had a 7 A.M. class three times a week. The hard part was getting up day-before-yesterday to get to class on time. I stumbled to class in the dark, half asleep, many a morning. Once I got there it wasn't so bad. A beautiful and magnificently stacked young lady occupied the seat just in front of me. Occasionally she would wear a sweater that looked just like my pajama tops. One morning, during a five-minute stretch break, the young lady smiled and said:

"Good morning."

I ignored the greeting and, looking quizzically at her, said, loud enough for half the class to hear, "I do wish you wouldn't wear my pajama tops to class.

She gasped and pretended to look shocked. The kids laughed or simply giggled. When class was dismissed, the young lady turned to me as she was putting on her coat and said in a voice loud enough to be heard throughout the room, "OK, I promise. I won't wear your pajama top to class anymore."

"Oh, that's alright," I replied. "I don't mind you wearing them— it's just that you're stretching the front all out of shape."

The class roared and she feigned shock, but you could tell it made her day.

I was talking to a friend who transferred from a large university in the East not long ago. He told me the following story:

Before the advent of the flower children and equality for all, the fraternities and sororities were great social institutions. Today, on most campuses, the Greek society is slowly decaying.

There was a time when fraternal wars were a natural part of campus life. Tempers would wax warm and it was a challenge to see which house could do the most damage to its rivals down the street— short of actual physical violence.

At one school, in the Southeastern part of the nation, the feuds got started unusually early. The second Sunday morning of the fall semester found a miserable, dejected, rickety old donkey tied to the brass door-knocker of the school's most prominent social fraternity— let's call them the *Signa Phi Nothin's.*

The ass was discovered when his raucous braying, about daybreak, roused the slumbering members. Of course this was an outrage and called for retaliatory action. Obviously this was the lowbrow work of those less than desirables down the strip, as Greek Row was called. *Signa Phi Nothin,* and *Tapa Kega Day* had long been rivals and friendly enemies.

The Tapa Kegs put out a guard and sat up nights waiting for the inevitable revengers. Sunday night passed— nothing happened. Monday was a carbon copy of the same thing. Wednesday, and still nothing. "Well," thought the Tapa Kegs, maybe they didn't suspect us after all. The weekend came and the Tapa Kegs kept a wary eye, but peace prevailed.

Then, Sunday morning it happened; "Wah-eh-eh-eh-eh, wah-eh-eh-eh-e-e-e. This music was accompanied by the gaggling clatter of a nude rooster. Furious that they had been taken in, duped, outsmarted, the whole house turned out. There, tied to the door, was their sorry-looking ass painted green, with their insignia in white letters on his ribby side. And his accomplice in the crime was a plucked rooster; painted red and tethered to the donkey's foreleg.

En masse, the fraternity marched up the street to the Signa Phi Nothin house where they were confronted by the entire occupancy of that establishment— clubs and bricks in hand.

Trouble would have ensued, for sure, but the Signa Phi housemother called the cops. Squad cars arrived and blocked the street. Both groups swelled around and shouted insults at one another and finally the Tapa Kegs were persuaded to retreat. The fact they were outnumbered two to one may have had some influence on the decision.

Three weeks passed and the Signa Phi Nothins kept such a tight guard on their place that nothing happened. The inactivity had its effect and finally the Signa Phis withdrew their guard. The next morning their entire basement was flooded to the windows.

Again war was imminent, and again the police prevailed. Weeks passed and no countermeasures were taken. And after long, tedious nights of alternating watch-duty, the Tapa Kegs let their guard down. The next morning their front and back doors were blocked with tons of manure— and it was raining. Their yard was ankle deep in the fragrant heaps. Later it was discovered that the fraternity president's car was full of the oozy stuff.

The fraternity was conveniently renamed the Barnyard Betas. The school, the town, and even the student senate stepped in and requested a halt, a ceasefire, before someone got hurt. An armistice was drawn up and both houses were forced to sign. A hostile truce ensued.

"I was sorry to see the armistice," my new friend said. "While I had not been involved in the pleasantries, I had thoroughly enjoyed the ingenuity and creative aspects of the situation."

Time dragged on with nothing to entertain it. The usual parties and such continued, but no real imaginative efforts were extended. "One day I was sitting in the Student Center sipping coffee and pretending to study when my ears began picking up bits and fragments of the conversation at the next table," my friend continued. "Thanksgiving was coming up and it seemed the fraternity (they were the Signa Phi Nothins) needed eleven turkeys to feed their flock for Thanksgiving dinner. At first it seemed like rather uncolorful, uneventful information. Unfortunately, I was born with the devious mind of a Chinese lawyer, and the more I mulled and processed that bit of trivia the more interesting it got. I turned around and spoke to the group, for I was acquainted with some of them:

" 'I couldn't help overhearing you boys,' I said. 'If you need some turkeys, why not get the turkeys and have some fun, too?'

"*Fun* being the key word to any college student's life, they were eager to listen. I told them that there was a turkey farm a few miles south of town. Why didn't they go down there and buy the desired number of turkeys, then send their uninformed pledges down to the farm at midnight to *steal* the turkeys? Once the pledges were in the barn grabbing turkeys, why, the owner could come out and fire a couple of shotgun blasts into the air and give the boys a good scare."

It was an idea that struck them as their type of humor. They thought it was the best thing since sex.

That night, in a local watering place, our friend saw some members of Tapa Kega fraternity who happened to be quenching their considerable thirst. Our friend joined them at their table, and by judicious maneuvering got the conversation around to the upcoming Thanksgiving holidays. Then he dropped it on them:

"You know, I heard today that the Signa Phi Nothins are buying eleven birds from the turkey farm down here south of town. They're gonna send their pledges out at dead midnight and the pledges think their gonna *steal* those turkeys! The old man who owns the farm is gonna come out and fire a couple of shots in the air with his shotgun and yell at 'em and give em a good scare."

"That's a great idea," said one of the Tapa Kegas, "— hell, I sure wish we could screw up their plan somehow!"

"Yeah," said another, "that'd be great!"

"Well-l-l," our friend said, "there *might* be a way, for some enterprising group to do that."

"How?" They were leaning over the table, hanging on the next words.

"Well, you fellas might consider sending *your* pledges down there 'bout, say, eleven. The owner would only think it was the Phi Nothins comin' a little early. You could take as many birds as you wanted, then, you know, kinda stir up the rest of them so's they would be real restless when the Nothins get there a while later."

". . . Hell-l-l-l yes!" they cried. "Fantastic! By God, we'll *do* it! Hey, thanks a lot!"

"Don't mention it," replied our friend as they left to seek another watering place.

A few nights later was the chosen time. The president of Tapa Kega Day posted a notice for a house meeting for 7 P.M. After the dinner hour, members and pledges gathered in the large chapter room. The president explained the situation to the enthusiastic members. And an order was given that nobody was to leave the house until the pledges left at ten forty-five for their rendezvous with the turkeys.

Since everyone was confined to quarters, extra rations of beer were prescribed and more kegs were tapped. By ten forty-five it was exceedingly drunk throughout the house. Still, it was time to go, so the pledges were poured into vehicles and driven the short distance to the turkey farm.

The cars were parked to the side of the road, near a culvert and a small creek. The pledges, smoking, cursing and making a good deal of noise, for they knew they had nothing to fear, tromped across a freshly plowed field toward the tin sheds where the turkeys were kept.

In their drunken clumsiness they tore a door off its hinges, a deed guaranteed not to charm the owner, who of course heard them. He was considerably surprised, too, for the young thieves were not expected for another hour. The owner sneaked out a side door of the house and stood waiting and somewhat annoyed with himself for agreeing to participate in such a venture.

Meanwhile the Tapa Kega pledges were inside the turkey barns trying to catch turkeys. It didn't take long for the turkeys to get roused up and excited about strangers being in their midst. Finally the pledges got their quota of turkeys, two apiece— there were sixteen pledges.

The farmer could tell from the shouts and profanity that the boys were tanked. And from the sounds he suspected he was losing more turkeys than the chapter had paid for. It irked him, but there was nothing to do about it now. "Boys will be boys, I guess," he thought.

As the boys came out of the barn, the farmer stood up and shouted:

"Hey . . . what's goin' on out there!" BOOM!— a shotgun blast ripped the air.

"Get outa there!" he hollered again.

BLAST! Another shot went off.

From out of the dark came a voice: "Aw, shut up you old fart!" and a rock whizzed past the farmer's head. Then a dirt-clod smashed against the house behind him; another rock broke a window.

The farmer was mad now, and sorely wanted to shoot somebody. From out of the dark came another voice: "Yeah, go on back in the house, you old bastard!"

The farmer raised his reloaded double-barrel to fire a warning shot over their heads but an egg— a turkey egg— caught him in the chest and splattered over his overalls and bare shoulders, for he had on no shirt. He fired the shot— a little lower than he would have moments before, and the intruders were gone.

The farmer propped up the barn door as best he could and returned to the house to take a bath and turn in. The more he thought about the situation and those smart-mouthed kids, the less he liked it.

Tapa Kega's pledges returned to their cars, loaded the plunder of the night and drove off.

Forty minutes later a black Chevy topped the hill north of the turkey farm. There were no lights and the engine was shut off instantly. The car coasted silently down to the culvert by the creek. Soon another car topped the rise, killed its engine, and coasted quietly down behind the first. Two more automobiles, following the same procedure, joined the first pair. Doors opened and hardly a sound escaped as the contents of the cars climbed out. Everybody was dressed in dark clothes— all twenty-three of them. These were the thieves from Signa Phi Nothin.

Quietly they picked their way down the bank and trecked into the dark and up the tiny creek. Previous reconnaissance had been done and it was discovered that a small dry ditch branched off from the creek and made its way to within less than a hundred yards of the tin barns.

The stealth and quietness of the group was amazing, for they had heard vague rumors that the man who operated the farm was a son-of-a-bitch.

A head popped up at the end of the ditch. Everything seemed safe, and soon nineteen crouching forms were creeping toward the turkey barns. (Four men were left with the cars.)

"We made it to the barn with no trouble," one of the turkey thieves said later. "One of the guys lifted the catch and pulled gently on the door . . . and the thing tried to fall over on us! We caught it and stood there holding our breath and that damn door. Nothing happened so we laid the door down and went in the barn. It was darker than the inside of a cow in there." The kid stopped for a pause and another took up the tale.

"Like he says we got inside and it was darker'n the inside o' your hat," said the kid who was majoring in animal science. "Well, sir, I been 'round chickens some, but I learned somethin' 'bout turkeys that night . . . spookiest damned birds you ever did see. If I didn't know better I'd a swore someone had been there and scared 'em up just afore we got there. Them birds begin to make a right smart of noise soon's we got inside. We felt around some an' when the first guy got his hands on a turkey's leg, why all hell goes an' breaks loose! I got knocked flat o' my back by a flyin' turkey— couldn't see him comin' you know— got myself up just in time to meet another'n head on an' went down again, an' got gagged on a feather. But I got myself ahold of one and beat it from there, fer I knew with all the noise we'uz makin' that trouble wasn't long in comin'. Well I was runnin' along toward the door, doing the best I could an' carrying that ole' gobbler, when I tripped over something. I lost my turkey, but there was plenty of 'em runnin around so's I just reached out and grabs me another'n and gits up and was streaking it fur the door when I runs inta somebody. We both fell down and got tangled up and couldn't hardly get away from one another."

"Outside," continued the agriculture student, "we heard a screen door slam and some feller a cussin' an' raisin' hell. You could tell without listening real close that he was mad. Then a shotgun went off and that helped us git untangled a mite faster. I was still determined to git me a turkey. I swung out in the dark and grabbed one. I got him by the wing and the durn fool near beat me to death with the other wing; and scratch? Them things has got strong feet you know."

"Well sir, I finally got one hand around his feet, like, so's he couldn't claw me, an' got my arm around his neck so's he couldn't peck me in the eye, and I lit out fer the door agin. I was in dead earnest this time cause I knew there was a madman out there somewhere!"

"I made it through the door and turned north along the barn. I was bearing down right hard, 'cause I wanted some real estate 'tween me'n him. 'Bout that time another shot was fired and a load of buckshot slammed into that tin barn. I'd a swore it was right behind me. I dropped that damned ole turkey, 'cause suddenly I wasn't as proud of him as I had been a minute before. Besides, I figured carrying him was shorting up my stride and I could use all the distance I could get 'long about then."

"Purty soon I was tearing along over that new plowed field. And I tell you fellers there ain't nothing like trying to run faster over ridges on a black night when you're dead skeert! Well, I was trucking along, runnin' over them plowed ridges thinking 'Gawd! I'll bet nobody's ever run this fast in all history.' Then Henry, there, passed me up, with a turkey in each hand, and ran on inta the dark. It was demoralizin'."

All week I had been worried about the paper that was due Friday. It was a feature-writing class in journalism; one of those classes taught by a professor who was technically excellent and mentally sterile. The subject for the feature was "What to do With Modifiers." In other words, this dull turnip wanted a class, supposedly training to write for newspapers, to write features on adjectives and adverbs. Art Buchwald would be hard pressed to come up with such a feature.

All week I had tried to get a substantial grip on the subject and nail it down. But, to me, the subject had all the form and substance of a fog. It would be the first time I had failed to turn in a paper. If I missed, what to do?

My friend in English, that's who I would call. She was a teaching assistant, a bright one. One of the few bright ones. She was also blonde and six feet three inches tall. That's three inches taller than me, but sometimes I play for high stakes. We had been out together on a few occasions. The phone was ringing.

"Hello?" It was a sleepy voice.

Without identifying myself, I said "How'd you like to make a fast twenty bucks tonight?"

There was a short pause, then she said, "Why, Sundown, I wouldn't even hold *hands* for twice that much."

A friend with a swift reflexive sense of humor like that is worth having.

Students are a hard-working, fun-loving breed. They are also very forgiving, considering the national classroom average of poor instructing.

# 15

# Graduate School

There is an old saying about higher education. It states that, "as a student attains advanced degrees, he learns more and more about less and less, until finally he knows everything about nothing.

If you analyze that statement carefully for content, you may begin to suspect that it was originated by Hubert Humphrey, for it really doesn't say one whole heck of a lot. But then, Hubert is a former professor, you know.

Doubtless some (perhaps most) of the advanced degrees in the sciences are necessary. But advanced degrees in any art form such as writing, painting, or theater, only seem to distill out any creative juices the student might have had.

If you're a student in a nonscience field and you have *talent,* don't go to graduate school. Get to work. Work hard, but, for your own sake, don't let professors, void of any creative sense, influence you or your work. If you have real ability then, believe me, someone *good* in your field— someone making an *honest* living in your field— will recognize your abilities and take the time to help you. If, however, you have no talent, but are determined to stay in the field, by all means collect all the degrees you can— and teach!

# Conclusion

It has not been my intention to enlighten professors, as *most* of them are light enough anyway, by virtue of the hot air they contain, but rather to inform the taxpayer and other supporters of schools about the incompetence that abounds at the average institution.

By enlightening students about the real character of professors, perhaps some changes might begin to take place. For there is nothing the *average* prof fears more than a room full of enlightened kids. God help the poor professor who might have to redo those musty old notes. And what if students suddenly began to demand that a class be *interesting?* Think of the thousands of professors who would be out of a job! Think of the improvement of the level of education.

No, what we need are some enlightened students, and a short open season on professors. Don't worry, the good ones will survive.

Offhand I do not recall a book that offered a dedication at the end. But, as this volume was hampered in its progress by a discouraging love affair, may I be excused for taking the opportunity to offer a

POST DEDICATION

To the very beautiful woman who made this book possible. May God rest her eternal soul.

(Unfortunately, she is not yet dead.)